Free-Motion
QUILTING 101
Techniques & Patterns for Beginners

ASHLEY NICKELS

The Taunton Press

Text © 2019 by Ashley Nickels
Photographs © 2019 by Susan Burdick
Illustrations © 2019 by The Taunton Press, Inc.

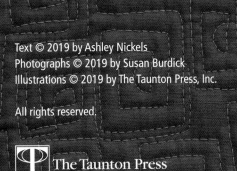

The Taunton Press, Inc., 63 South Main Street,
Newtown, CT 06470-2344
Email:tp@taunton.com

Editor: Carolyn Mandarano
Copy editor: Peter Chapman
Indexer: Barbara Mortenson
Jacket/Cover design: Barbara Cottingham
Interior design: Barbara Cottingham
Layout: Barbara Cottingham
Illustrator: Alexis Seabrook
Photographer: Susan Burdick, except p. 5 (bottom) by author
Residence location: Courtesy of Dave and Stephanie Sullivan

The following names/manufacturers appearing in *Free-Motion
Quilting 101* are trademarks: Adobe®, Aurifil®, Baby Lock®, Bernina®,
Dye-Na-Flow®, Elna®, Husqvarna Viking®, Jacquard®, Juki®, Kona®,
Kwik Klip™, Mettler®, Roxanne™, Schmetz®, Sharpie®, Singer®,
Spirograph®, Superior®, Supreme Slider™

Library of Congress Cataloging-in-Publication Data

  Names: Nickels, Ashley, author.
  Title: Free-motion quilting 101 : techniques & patterns for beginners /
    Ashley Nickels.
  Description: Newtown, CT : The Taunton Press, Inc., [2019] | Includes
index.
  Identifiers: LCCN 2019014737 | ISBN 9781641550024
  Subjects: LCSH: Machine quilting--Patterns. | Patchwork--Patterns. |
Machine quilting--Technique.
  Classification: LCC TT835 .N4925 2019 | DDC 746.46/041--dc23
  LC record available at https://lccn.loc.gov/2019014737

Printed in the United States of America
10 9 8 7 6 5 4 3 2 1

DEDICATION

To my first and favorite teacher:
my mom, Sue

ACKNOWLEDGMENTS

I'd like to first and foremost thank the team at Taunton Press: Lynne Phillips, Barb Cottingham, Susan Burdick, and especially Carolyn Mandarano, for all of the guidance and support during the process of writing this book. It was a pleasure to work with you, and I am grateful for the opportunity.

To anyone who found me on social media and has encouraged my writing, thank you.

To all of the artists and makers out there, thank you for pursuing your passions, as it has inspired me to pursue mine.

To my dear friends and trusted advisors: You motivate me to create and have supported me as an artist in countless ways. Thank you.

To my family, who believe in me fiercely and always encourage me to follow my dreams: Thank you.

And finally, to Heraclio, for inspiring me to dream big, and at the same time reminding me of what is truly important. Thank you.

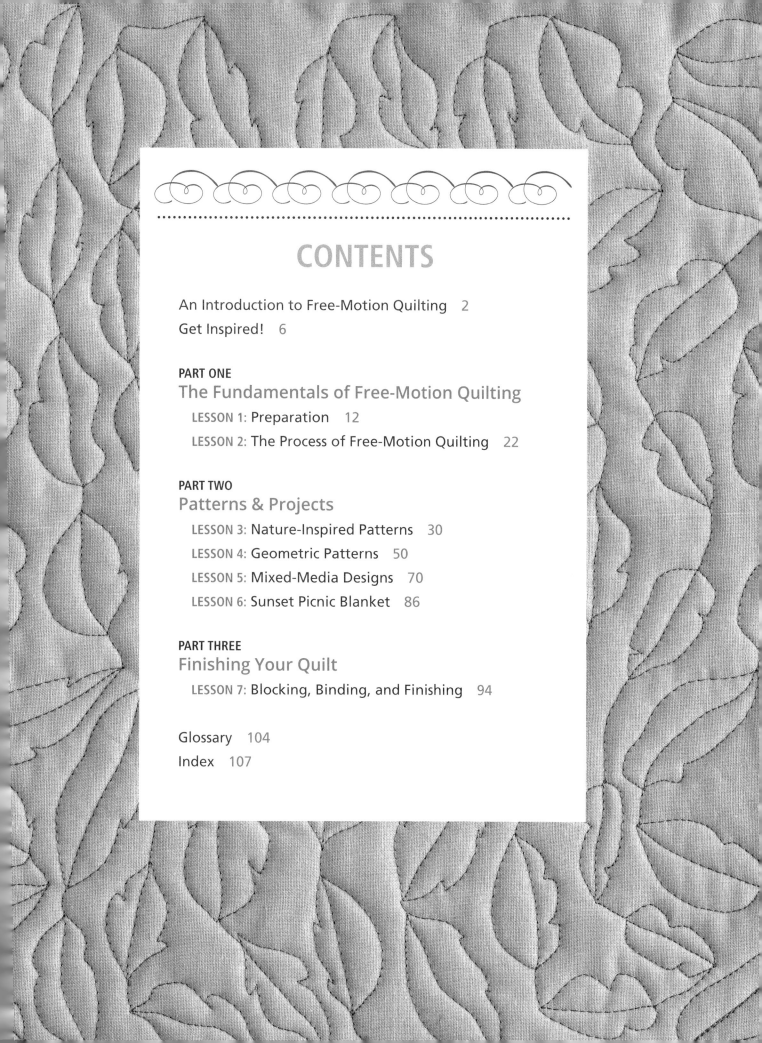

CONTENTS

AN INTRODUCTION TO FREE-MOTION QUILTING

I grew up surrounded by creative people, quilters and makers of various things. I made my first nine patch at age eight and was designing my own bags by high school. I love to sew, quilt, paint, write, travel, and generally be inspired.

My journey through life has been about learning but also about teaching, and for me, the two are woven together. I teach what I know and get inspired by those I teach to learn something else or to try something new. Although I have been a classroom teacher in my day job, I'm also a quilt teacher both online and in person. The teacher-student cycle is part of my never-ending journey of connecting the creative dots.

I'm always looking for something new to add to my quilting projects, and free-motion quilting provides that opportunity. In my mind, it's as essential to the quilting process as choosing a block design, picking fabrics, and piecing patchwork. I also love that free-motion quilting can add depth and dimension to a piece, whether in the form of a straight line, detailed pattern, or words. Quilting is the "cherry on top" of the quilt, enriching a piece created by your hand.

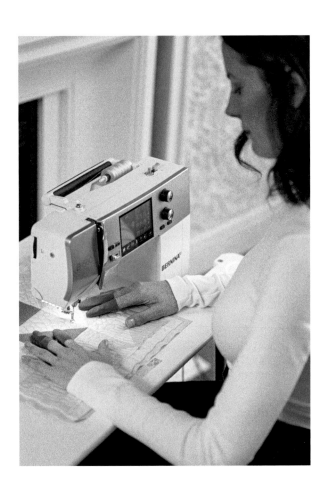

You might be one of the many quilters who thinks free-motion quilting is beyond your abilities, who doesn't know where to start or how to finish. But this is where practice and repetitive exercises come in, because practicing free-motion quilting is like practicing any other activity. A runner starts by running for five minutes at a time for weeks before

upping her distance. When learning a musical instrument, you might play simple chord sequences for weeks or even months before moving on to a song. A yoga practitioner can hold a pose for only thirty seconds at first. It's no wonder the quilter who has the expectation that she will quilt a bed-sized quilt upon her first attempt is paralyzed by the enormity of the task.

My teaching style and philosophy toward any creative endeavor is based on the idea that practice is developed over time and that it must be cultivated from within each of us. Use this book as if you were taking a class. With my guidance and step-by-step instruction on the techniques of free-motion quilting, combined with simple designs and a few projects that will allow you to dive in and quilt small-scale projects, the practice of free-motion quilting will not only become more manageable, but it will also be fun!

The Lesson Plan

Using the framework of teaching as a guide, I've called each "chapter" a lesson. Each is structured as a step-by-step plan to provide necessary information on how to learn free-motion quilting through a simple quilting design. Within each quilting design you'll find a practice page to help you warm up with pencil and paper before moving to the sewing machine. Usually, no one tells you to draw in a book—but I'm telling you to do just that! Working through repetitive drawing exercises will provide invaluable muscle

memory practice both for mind and hands. Because you don't mark a design on fabric in free-motion quilting, drawing the design will help you visualize a pattern before quilting it on the machine. And even though the tools for quilting and hand-drawing are different, you will learn to get comfortable drawing without lifting your pencil—and stitching at the machine without stopping and starting.

Starting at the beginning translates into the most successful end result, so the lessons in Part 1 provide an in-depth explanation of materials, fabric, supplies, machine setup, and more. In Part 2 you will find patterns and projects, each starting with instruction on working first on paper then moving to fabric by working on practice squares. The focus here is on three different styles of quilting from very basic to more advanced—nature patterns, geometric patterns, and mixed-media designs. Each style of quilting is followed by a small project—a tote bag, placemats, and a wall hanging—although the practice squares can also be finished. A larger picnic blanket project, which includes free-motion designs from each lesson, completes Part 2. Part 3 provides step-by-step instruction for finishing any quilt.

I've included Design Advice sidebars to help you explore other ideas when you're ready to try something new. I've also included a notation when a pattern is one of my students' favorites. I encourage you to perhaps try these designs first, with their tried-and-true instruction that will build your confidence as you learn free-motion quilting.

Finding Inspiration

Although I've provided you with simple quilting designs to get started, I encourage you to look around you every day for inspiration. For me, inspiration comes from nature, architectural details, a childhood memory, art museums, or even advertisements at the bus stop. When I feel connected to a design, I find that replicating it also adds a mindfulness to my work. The photos on these pages have provided inspiration to me.

The pages that follow include a gallery of a few of my favorite pieces. I hope these inspire you to explore your own style as you start your free-motion quilting journey.

Please keep in touch and share your designs and inspiration: @alphabetashley (Instagram) and include hashtag #freemotion101.

Warmly,

Ashley

"PIXELS"

The geometric quilting technique in "Pixels" is based on the design of an iron gate in my neighborhood (see p. 5).

"WILL'S GALAXY"

Simple straight-line quilting is a nice option, as shown in this baby quilt.

"THE WATERCOLOR PLOT, 1"

In this watercolor quilt, I used black thread for high contrast and invisible thread to create subtle background textures.

"AMBROSIA OF THE WOODS"

The painted portion of this watercolor and pieced quilt takes center stage due to quilting with black thread.

PART ONE

The Fundamentals of Free-Motion Quilting

Lesson 1

PREPARATION

Getting ready for free-motion quilting is, in some ways, half the battle of free-motion quilting. Similar to the sentiments "unrolling your yoga mat is the hardest part" or "as long as I get myself to my easel, the rest is easy," getting your quilting project and your sewing machine set up is often the most challenging aspect to quilting. This doesn't mean that the actual quilting is a breeze, but it will be more fun and creative if you have everything you need at hand, before you start.

When I first started free-motion quilting, I didn't realize how important things like sewing machine setup, needle size, and thread weight would be. But once I began to notice what worked for me and why, and more importantly what did not work for me and why, I hit a tremendous stride—and started enjoying the process—that continues to this day.

In this first lesson, I will be saving you from all of my struggles! Here you'll learn the absolute essential tools to use for free-motion quilting, along with why they are critical, as well as how to set up your quilting project so you can dive into the fun part: making beautiful designs on your quilts.

Getting to Know Your Sewing Machine

The sewing machine is an incredible invention that has revolutionized how we quilt. These days, sewing machines are so technologically advanced that they can do our quilting for us. But while all the digital options and latest features are wonderful, it's important to learn the basics of quilting, and so I will teach those basics on a stripped-down, computerized machine. Much like learning to drive on a manual car instead of an automatic, learning to quilt based on traditional techniques will give you a better feel for your quilting, much more control of your work, and the satisfaction of quilting your own quilt without any assistance.

A common misconception about quilting is that you need a "fancy" machine in order to free-motion quilt. The truth is, any sewing machine will work! Lower-end machines have the capacity for free-motion quilting just like high-end machines, and you can spend anywhere between $150 and $10,000 for a machine that you can successfully quilt on. If you're buying a new machine, there are some features you should look for to make sure you're getting the best machine for your type of quilting and budget, such as the ability to lower the feed dogs, the ability to adjust tension easily, and a straight-stitch throat plate option, shown below. Also, make sure you have good dealer support in case you need to ask machine-specific questions.

See the chart on p. 14 for sewing machine brand comparisons.

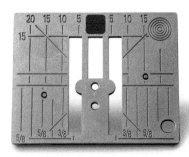

The straight-stitch throat plate is an option for more advanced quilters. The single hole prevents the quilt layers from getting pushed into the machine, improving stitch quality.

Sewing Machines

Entry-level machines often come with a feed dog cover, instead of a lever or button that lowers the feed dogs out of sight. Higher-end machines offer computerized screens and a large space to sew. Another note about brands: Quilters tend to be loyal to their preferred brand. I use Bernina machines for free-motion quilting.

BRAND	COST	COMMENTS
Baby Lock	$-$$$	Recently began focusing on quilting machines; offers great options
Bernina	$$-$$$$	Swiss-made, high-quality machines; my preferred machines for free-motion quilting
Brother	$	Good value—the CS6000i is an affordable entry-level machine
Elna	$-$$	Good range of quilting-specific machines
Janome	$-$$$	Very popular brand, great support and community
Juki	$-$$$	First company to offer the sit-down longarm
Pfaff	$-$$$	Quality machines since 1862
Singer	$-$$	American company; good entry-level machines
Husqvarna Viking	$-$$$	Reliable company and machines

Feed dogs

Feed dogs are the metal "claws" that are designed to pull your quilt from front to back. In order to free-motion quilt, you'll need to drop the claws. On many machines, you'll press a button to drop the feed dogs. Some machines have a plastic plate that you put over them. Consult your machine's manual for instructions.

Sewing machine maintenance

Most manufacturers recommend that you service your machine every year, and that you oil it regularly. I put a few drops of oil near the bobbin area every few weeks. If your machine has not been serviced in a while, I recommend taking it to a local dealer/service shop to get it tuned up. While you're there, make sure you ask them to show you where and how to oil your machine.

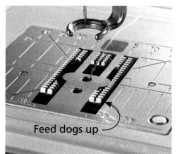

Feed dogs up

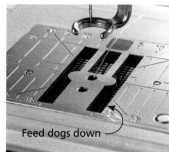

Feed dogs down

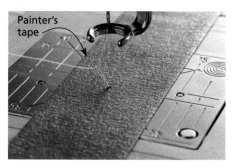

Painter's tape

On some machines, such as some older Singer-brand Featherweight machines, you can't do either. In this case, I usually add a few layers of thick painter's tape over the feed dogs and poke a hole for the needle; this works like a charm.

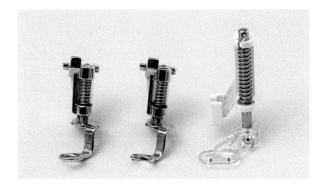

Presser feet

Free-motion quilting requires a darning foot, or what is often referred to as a "quilting foot" or a "free-motion quilting foot." These feet are designed with a spring, and do not apply pressure on the quilt top, allowing complete and full movement while sewing.

Darning feet generally come in the "open" or "closed" variety. Any of them will work, though my preference is an "open-toe darning foot" because it gives me full visibility of my stitches. I use the #24 foot for my Bernina machine.

The walking foot attachment, while not used for free motion, is often used for straight-line quilting and stitching in the ditch. Oftentimes, quilters will secure their quilts with straight lines before doing any free-motion quilting.

Extended base

Most sewing machines come with an extended base attachment. This provides more flat surface around the presser foot. The more flat surface on the same plane as your presser foot, the less your quilt will fall off the edge of your sewing surface. When part of the quilt falls off the edge, the weight will begin to pull the rest of the quilt down, which may inevitably distort your stitches.

Preparing your sewing space

Your sewing space and how you set it up is also an important factor in the success of your quilting. Here are a few recommendations:

- **Place a long table at the end of your sewing surface.** This will allow your quilt to fall off the edge of your sewing machine and sewing surface, but only a few inches to the table. The bigger the quilt, the longer the table should be.
- **Use a table designed to fit a sewing machine.** There are many on the market. Because I have a small studio, I use the SewEzi table, which also serves as a travel table (it is collapsible and has wheels).
- **For bigger quilts,** set up an ironing board behind you to catch the weight of the quilt.

Tools, Notions, and Other Essentials

There are lots of different notions and tools available at your local quilt shop and online. When you're first starting out, don't mistakenly think you need one of everything! Below you'll find information on must-have notions as well as nice-to-have notions and tools. As you spend more time quilting, you'll discover what works for you.

Thread

Thread is an essential part of quilting, so it is important to educate yourself about different threads. Threads come in different weights and ply and different materials.

All threads have a specific strength (measured in weight) and ply, both represented in numbers. For weight, the lower the number, the thicker the thread. For example, a 40-weight thread is thicker than a 60-weight thread. Many silk threads are 100 weight, which is super thin. When buying thread, note that the weight is first, followed by the ply; for example, 50-weight 3-ply thread will read as 50/3.

For ply, threads are usually 2 or 3 ply. If your thread is 2 ply, this means that there are two fibers twisted together to create your thread, and if it is 3 ply, there are three fibers. So, a 50-weight 2-ply thread and a 50-weight 3-ply thread are the same strength, but a slightly different thickness. The 3-ply

thread will show up in your quilting as a thicker line and will stand out more than the 2 ply.

Generally speaking, if your quilting fabric is cotton and your batting is a cotton blend, it is recommended that you use cotton thread for quilting. This keeps your materials consistent, particularly if you will be washing your quilts. Because every material reacts slightly differently to water, using cotton fibers consistently in your quilt means that your fabric and thread will all shrink at the same rate, preventing any bunching or distortion.

I prefer to use 100% cotton thread for this reason, and I rarely use polyester thread for my quilting (see the sidebar on the facing page). But another reason I use cotton thread is because it is soft and it creates beautiful stitches.

My choice for quilting is the Aurifil 50/2. Aurifil is quite subtle on the quilt surface yet is sturdy and resilient. Another big reason I use Aurifil is the availability of a broad color palette. You can purchase the color card online and use it to match your threads beautifully.

An embroidery or silk thread (60+ weight threads) creates beautifully soft quilting designs, and the 40-weight threads (Aurifil and King Tut) can be excellent choices for either a quilt you know will get heavy use (like a baby quilt or a picnic blanket) or for quilting that you want to stand out and highlight.

Left to right: Aurifil 50/2, Mettler Silk Finish 50/3, Superior King Tut 40/3.

Common Thread Choices

THREAD TYPE	FINISH	BEST USE	COST
Aurifil 50/2	Subtle, smooth	Any quilt, particularly for subtle quilting	$$
Aurifil 40/2	Thick, smooth	Any quilt, quilting will be bolder	$$
Mettler Silk Finish	Sturdy, smooth	Great for piecing, and quilting any quilt	$
Superior MasterPiece	Sturdy, subtle	Any quilt	$$
Superior King Tut	Bold, sturdy	For bold quilting, quilts that will get heavy use	$$
Mettler Embroidery	Smooth, shiny	Embroidery details on wall-hanging quilts	$$

What Can Go Wrong with Thread

PROBLEM	POSSIBLE CAUSES	SOLUTION
Thread breaks often	Bobbin thread is too heavy.	Check the bobbin thread and use 50/3 or 50/2 (not 40).
	Cheap thread	Try a different thread.
	Wrong needle size	Check you are using the correct size for your thread choice.
	Top thread is not threaded properly.	Stop and rethread.
	Machine needs oiling.	Put a few drops into the bobbin area.
Skipped stitches	Dull needle	Start over: 1. Rethread your top thread. 2. Change the sewing machine needle to the correct size. 3. Oil the bobbin area. 4. Use a regular foot, raise the feed dogs, and sew straight lines on a scrap before sewing your project.

A note on invisible thread

As a die-hard cotton-thread quilter, I steer clear of most polyester threads. However, I love to occasionally use clear plastic polyester thread, otherwise known as *invisible* thread, in a lot of my watercolor quilts. Why use invisible thread? As the name says, the thread is barely noticeable, and it creates texture and depth without highlighting your stitches. I use it on quilts that have areas of heavy quilting with black thread to create visual breathing room. It is also handy because you don't have to worry about thread-matching your background fabric.

I use YLI brand invisible thread because it is durable and strong. When quilting with invisible thread on the top, I use a muslin-colored Aurifil 50/2 in the bobbin.

There is no right or wrong thread. If you like, start with my favorites or even the current trend, but don't be afraid to try different threads until you come up with the right combination for your desired effect and how your quilt will be used.

Top vs. Bobbin There are two places on your machine that need thread. The top thread, as it is referred to, will be the thread that will appear on the top of your quilt. The bobbin thread will show up on the back of your quilt. The bobbin is found underneath your presser foot; see your machine's manual on how to thread a bobbin.

For consistency, I use cotton thread in the top and bobbin, and, in general, I use the same thread in both. I say in general because often if I'm using a 50/3 thread, I'll still use an Aurifil 50/2 in the bobbin. Also, I *do not* recommend using a 40-weight thread in the bobbin, as I find it does not flow as smoothly. If you are using 40 weight for the top thread to create those thick and luscious quilting designs, I recommend using 50/3 in the bobbin.

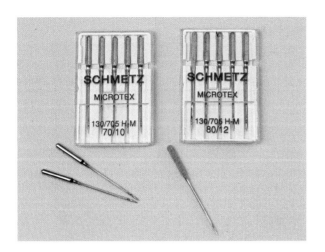

Match Thread to Needle Size

NEEDLE SIZE	THREAD TYPE	RECOMMENDED THREAD SIZES
90/14	Heavier	King Tut 40/3
80/12	Average weight	Mettler and Masterpiece 50/3 cotton Aurifil 40/2
70/10	Finer	Aurifil 50/2 cotton Mettler 60/2 Invisible thread Can be used for 100-weight silk threads
60/8*	Silk	100-weight silk threads

*The 60/8 is a fragile needle. For a beginner who would like to use thin silk thread, I recommend the 70/10 needle. Leave the 60/8 to more experienced quilters.

Needles

Needles and thread are very closely connected. The weight of your thread will determine which needle size to use. If you don't use the right-size needle for the weight of thread you're using, your stitch quality will suffer greatly.

All quilters have their preferences for type of quilting needle, and my preferred needles are the Schmetz brand Microtex Sharp needles. You can find them at most quilt stores as well as online, and they come in all different sizes.

Batting

There are many different battings on the market, each with a different loft and weight. I generally use the same batting (80/20 blend) whether I am making a small quilt, a large quilt, or a small project like a bag or placemat. The larger the quilt, the heavier the overall quilt will be, so a cotton/poly blend offers a more lightweight option. For the most part, 100% cotton battings do not give quilts as much body. I encourage you to try out different battings to see which work for you.

Change your sewing machine needle

You should change your needle after *every 5 to 6 hours of quilting.* Yes, you read that correctly. That means that if you are quilting all day for a few days in a row, you need to change your needle every day! Oftentimes, when your machine starts skipping stitches or your tension begins to get wonky, a dull needle is the culprit. Do not skimp on your sewing machine needles! They are about $1 each and are a worthy investment.

Choosing Batting

TYPE	LOFT	PROS	CONS
100% cotton	Low	Natural fibers, breathes well	Shrinks 3-5%, high-density batting creates dense quilt
Cotton/poly blends (80/20, 50/50)	Low to medium	Lightweight, versatile, easy to find	Some shrinkage
Bamboo	Low	Natural fibers, eco-friendly; made from fast-growing tree	Harder to find
Wool and wool blend	Low to medium	Natural insulator, comes in black	Some people find wool itchy, loft can be inconsistent
Polyester	Medium to high	Durable, resistant to moths and mildew, easy to find	Synthetic fibers, therefore low breathability

Rubber-glove fingertips

When you lower the feed dogs to start quilting you will be completely in charge of moving the quilt. To do this, you need to be able to grip the quilt surface. Our fingertips are often too slippery to gain good control. Quilt gloves, similar to gardening gloves, are designed to give your hands more grip because they have rubbery nubs on the fingertips.

But my "grippers of choice" are even simpler than that. I like to buy rubber gloves at the supermarket (the ones designed for dishwashing) and cut off the index and middle fingers to use on each hand (see the bottom photo on p. 23). I have found that four rubber fingers—two on each hand—do the trick!

Curved-tip scissor snips

My technique for free-motion quilting involves snipping threads very close to the surface of the quilt top. For this, a pair of snips, particularly the curved-tip variety, is super handy. The curved tip allows the scissor to cut as close to the quilt as possible, thus keeping your quilt top smooth and flat.

Marking pencil

Although I do not use a lot of marking in free-motion quilting, I still rely on a marking pencil to mark boundaries or to outline certain shapes. My marking pencil of choice is the gray Quilter's Choice by Roxanne. I like this pencil because it is thick and can make a generous and heavy line, yet it is chalk-based, so markings are easy to remove, either with a damp cloth or when laundered.

Curved safety pins

On pp. 20–21, you'll learn my technique for basting. I use pins, and I prefer the 1-in. curved variety. How many you'll need depends entirely on the size of your quilt. In general, I place one pin every 3 in. to 4 in.

Hand needle and thread

The last step in basting your quilt involves a hand-basted stitch around the perimeter. For this, you'll need a regular sewing needle and thread.

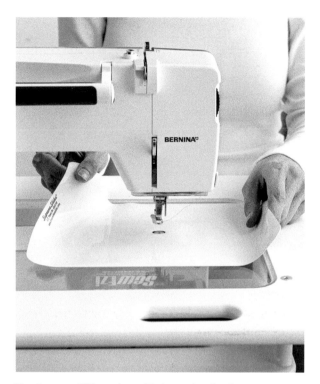

The Supreme Slider reduces friction and makes free-motion quilting smoother.

Supreme Slider

Many quilters use the Supreme Slider to help ease the flow of their machine quilting. This is a Teflon sheet that you lay over your sewing machine base to cut down on the friction between the machine and fabric. Take caution, however, as this slippery surface can actually work *for* gravity and *against you,* and with bigger, heavier quilts, using this sheet may actually cause pulling and distortion.

Kwik Klip

This tool will help you during the pin-basting process. The Kwik Klip allows you to close the safety pins easily, as it is designed to grab onto the pin to ease the closing process. A DIY alternative to this would be a grapefruit spoon!

Painter's tape or masking tape

Use tape during the basting process to tape your backing fabric to the floor. This keeps it in place while you are pin-basting.

Preparing Your Project for Quilting

Before you begin quilting, it's very important that you secure the three layers of the quilt (the top, the batting, and the backing fabric). This is deliciously referred to as the quilt sandwich. To secure—or baste—your quilt sandwich, there are various techniques you can use. If you have an outdoor space, spray-basting can be a good option. However, I prefer the pin-basting technique because I don't love the smell of the spray-basting adhesive. Plus, you can pin-baste indoors and not worry about the fumes.

The importance of basting is often overlooked by quilters because doing it right is tedious. However, I can assure you that it is one of the most critical steps to the quilting process. When you begin quilting, it is natural (and necessary!) to pull, tug, fold, and roll your quilt often. If your quilt is not basted securely, you run the risk of distorting your quilt, which can create ripples, folds, and even waves in your quilt. It pays to be diligent and take your time.

Pin-basting 101

Follow the steps here to ensure you pin-baste your quilt correctly.

1. Lay your backing fabric right side down on a flat surface. Flatten it with your hands and place a piece of masking or painter's tape every 5 in. to 6 in. Take care not to pull or tug on the fabric. **(A)**

2. Place the batting on top of the backing fabric. The backing fabric should be an inch or two larger all around. Take care to smooth out any bumps or lumps and remove any threads that may have gotten stuck. Batting is a magnet for fibers! **(B)**

3. Place your quilt top right side up on top of the batting. The batting and backing fabric should be at least 2 in. to 3 in. larger than the quilt top. Smooth out any bumps or lumps and take care not to pull or distort the fabric. **(C)**

4. Begin to place the pins, leaving 3 in. to 4 in. between them. I like to begin by placing pins at the center of the X/Y axis and then move outward in all four directions. I'll go back and fill in each quadrant from center to the edge. Leave each pin open after inserting it through the layers—you'll close all of the pins at the end. **(D)**

5. With all the pins in place, it's time to close them, following the same order in which you placed them. Feel free to use the Kwik Klip or a grapefruit spoon to assist in closing the pins. **(E)**

6. Finally, make a basting stitch with your needle and thread along the perimeter of your quilt, approximately ¼ in. from the edge. Stitches can be large and "chunky," and you can put a couple of stitches on your needle at a time to expedite the process. I generally use a different thread color than my quilt top material so that it stands out. **(F)**

7. Remove the tape and you're ready to quilt. **(G)**

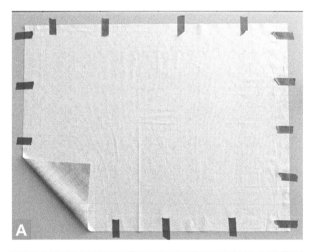

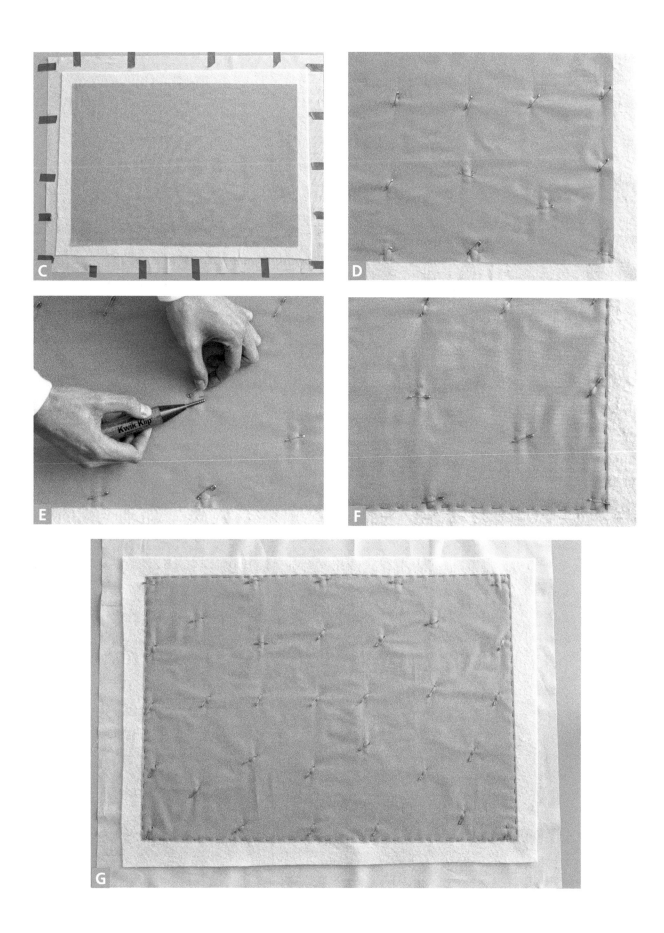

Lesson 2

THE PROCESS OF FREE-MOTION QUILTING

Free-motion quilting can be as exhilarating as it sounds. The freedom! But just like getting behind the wheel of a car for the first time and actually driving somewhere, using your sewing machine to free-motion quilt takes some practice. The first steps will be to understand where to put your hands, how to hold the quilt, and how to start and stop so that your threads don't come undone. Don't worry, though. I'll teach you everything you need to know to build your confidence and make the experience fun.

Security stitches   Regular stitches

Getting Started
Body position

How you grip or hold your quilt is very important for the outcome of your stitches. But more than any-thing, finding an ergonomic position for your hands, arms, and body will allow you to avoid injuries that might keep you from your favorite hobby.

First, sit up straight and relax your shoulders, making sure you don't hunch forward. If your chair/table combo is forcing you to hunch your shoulders, consider putting your table on risers or changing your chair height.

Next, position your arms so they make an "L" shape and your forearms are relaxed. Keep your shoulders relaxed—don't shrug them up toward your ears.

Finally, place your hands and fingers on your quilt, keeping them flat and open. As tempting as it can be to grip with your hands and fingers, maintaining a lighter touch as you work will be more comfortable and provide a better outcome.

Security stitches

One of the beautiful advantages of free-motion quilting is that you never have to bury your starting and stopping stitches in the back of your quilts. In order to keep your quilting firmly fixed, you need to make a series of security stitches each time you start—and stop—quilting. Here is the process.

1. Put on your rubber-glove fingertips.

2. With your machine threaded and the needle in the up position, locate the starting point of your quilting under the needle and lower the presser foot. Then, either using your machine's hand crank on the right side or a button that raises or lowers the needle, lower the needle and then bring it back up again.

3. Lift the presser foot and tug on the top thread. This will pull the bobbin thread through to the quilt top.

4. Once you have both the top and bobbin threads in your hands, lower the needle in the exact spot where those threads are coming from. This is the first security stitch.

5. Following the quilting design, make a series of three to four tiny security stitches right next to each other. You must move your quilt in order to make these security stitches. Sewing in place will only create a knot in the back of your quilt.

6. Now you're ready to quilt the regular-length stitches to create your design. (See p. 26 for more about stitch length.)

7. Once you've sewn an inch or so, pause with the needle down and clip the loose threads as close to the quilt top as possible.

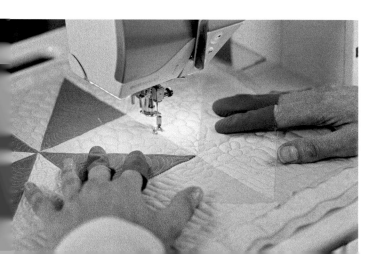

Any time you need to stop quilting, whether at the end of a section or mid-design to make any sort of adjustment, you'll need to also use security stitches and clip your threads. When you approach the end of a section, simply sew 3 to 4 tiny stitches just like the ones you began with. Now you can take the quilt away from the machine and clip the top and back threads as close to the quilt top as possible, using those curved-edge scissors or snips. There is no need to pull the back thread through to the front.

How to move your quilt (and how not to)

Once you've honed your hand placement and have made your security stitches, it's time to put this quilt into gear! Although you have complete control and freedom when free-motion quilting, it's important to keep yourself centered.

Regardless of how large or small your quilting project or how simple or difficult your quilting design, it's best to quilt in sections. If you're working on a bed quilt, you'll want to "package" it as you work so that the backing fabric doesn't pucker (for more on this, see p. 27). Think of your square (or rectangular) quilt as a map, having a north, south, east, and west. As you move through your quilting, make sure that during one continuous quilting section your north, south, east, and west stay in the same position. This

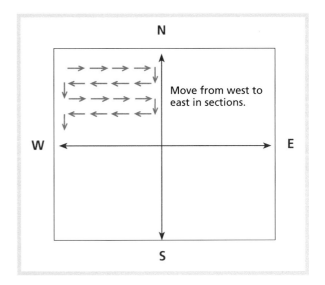
Move from west to east in sections.

does not mean you cannot move from California to New Jersey, for example, but you need to move from west to east without pivoting your axis.

If you want to change your quilt's axis, be sure you stop with the needle down and then pivot the quilt. For larger quilts that are rolled and packaged for quilting, you'll have to take the quilt out of the machine and repackage it if you want to change direction.

Speed control

Pedal to the metal? 5 miles per hour? A lot of quilters wonder what the "right" speed is for machine quilting. The truth is that each quilter will develop her own comfort level with what speed works the best.

You'll also need to move the quilt yourself in order to get anywhere. The speed at which you move the quilt will be intimately connected to machine speed. Start by moving the quilt slowly. You're looking for a "not too fast but not too slow" pace, which will allow you to stop and start as needed. You'll get the feel for it the more you practice. Always remember to keep your quilt's axis—its north, south, east, and west—in the same position as you are moving.

Your Machine's Speed Dial vs. You Most machines have a dial that will adjust speed control. This is a great tool to use when you are teaching someone to sew for the first time. Over the years I have become

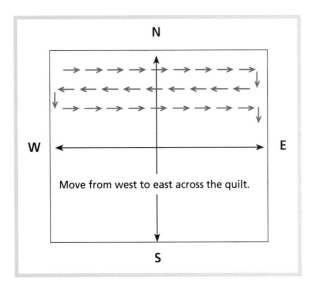
Move from west to east across the quilt.

the most comfortable having the speed dial cranked all the way to the right (or at the fastest speed) so that I can control my speed entirely with the foot pedal.

I recommend finding a speed that is neither too slow nor too fast. Too slow means that you are starting and stopping very frequently and that your quilting will not flow as well as if you have a little bit of speed going. (By flow, I'm referring to both the flow of the quilting and the smoothness of the stitches.) However, if you are sewing too fast, you run the risk of losing control of your design altogether.

I have found that often my speed will actually increase if I start sewing too fast, and then my body becomes tense and I start to have the "shopping cart down a hill" effect—my speed accelerates more and more until I've crashed into another design, or worse, I have to rip out the stitches and start over.

TIP How do you know when you've found the right speed? You'll know when you stop thinking about it. Experiment with speeding up, slowing down, and everything in between, and you'll land on your sweet spot.

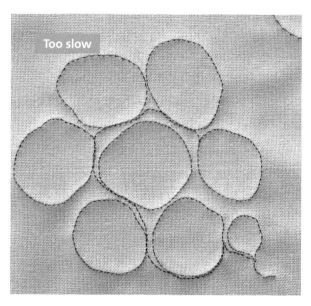

Too slow

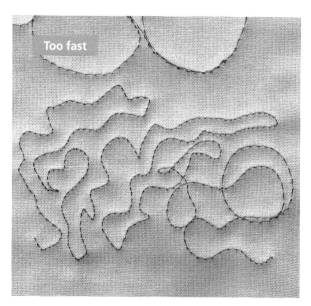

Too fast

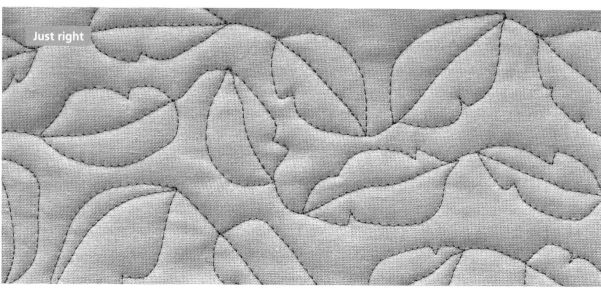

Just right

Stitch length

Finding the right balance between how fast you move your quilt and how fast you sew is the key to achieving a consistent stitch length. Once the feed dogs are dropped, it will be entirely up to you to move your quilt top. This can feel extremely liberating but at the same time quite daunting. Do not worry! Finding what works for you just takes practice.

Many quilters new to free-motion quilting want to know if there is an ideal stitch length. There isn't! It's more important that your quilting have a consistent stitch length, meaning that you more or less maintain the same stitch length—whether short or long—throughout your entire quilt.

Inconsistent stitch length

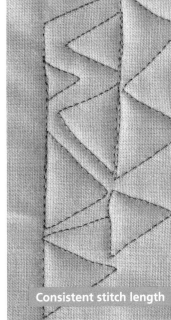
Consistent stitch length

Stitch regulator

A stitch regulator is a device that attaches to your sewing machine and controls the stitch length based on the number of stitches per inch you've set in the controls and how fast you are moving the quilt top. The regulator speeds up or slows down the machine based on these parameters.

There's no denying that a stitch regulator takes one factor out of the equation, leaving you to be able to focus more on your design. However, stitch regulators can be cost-prohibitive for many quilters, and many sewing machines do not come with the ability to incorporate this type of attachment. I recommend that you learn to quilt the old-fashioned way, with you as the regulator.

Tension

Machine quilting can definitely cause tension in your body, but your sewing machine's tension is a whole other story. Correct tension on your sewing machine refers to even stitching that looks the same on both the top and back of your quilt.

Before starting your quilting, you should test your machine's tension. An easy way to do this is to have contrasting thread colors for your top thread and your bobbin thread. This way, you'll be able to see if any bobbin thread is coming through from the back or if any top thread shows on the back. It is harder to determine tension issues if you use matching thread colors.

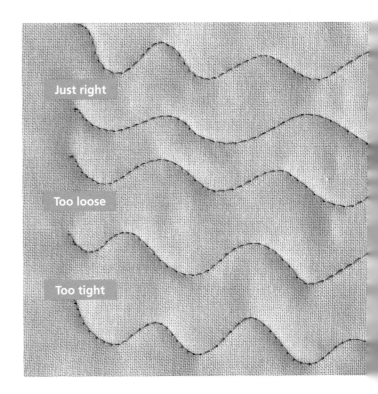
Just right

Too loose

Too tight

Top Tension The top tension, a.k.a. the tightness or looseness of your top thread, is controlled by a dial on your sewing machine.

You will know if the top tension is too tight because you will see small dots of bobbin thread coming through between the stitches on the quilt top. To fix top tension that is too tight, lower the tension dial in one-quarter increments at a time and then continue sewing to see if this fixes the problem. For example, if your tension dial is set to 4, lower it to 3.75 and keep sewing to see if that makes a difference. If it doesn't, lower it by another quarter increment and test again.

When top tension is too loose, you can see small dots of the top thread showing on the back of the quilt. To fix tension that is too loose, raise the tension dial in one-quarter increments. For example, if your tension is at 4, raise it to 4.25. Keep sewing and see if that makes a difference. If not, raise it by another quarter increment.

Bottom Tension In general, if the bottom tension is off, adjusting the top tension dial should do the trick. The bottom tension is associated with a tiny screw in your bobbin case. When you take your sewing machine for servicing, the mechanic will make sure that this tension screw is at the appropriate tightness. There is a way to adjust the bottom tension yourself, though it is recommended that only a sewing machine mechanic should adjust this tension for you.

If adjusting your top tension has not fixed the issue, nor has changing your needle, rethreading, or oiling your machine, it might be worth having a mechanic check out the bottom tension. For more information on adjusting sewing machine tension, see Ruth Ciemnoczolowski's article "How to Achieve Ideal Sewing Machine Thread Tension" at threadsmagazine.com.

TIP Before adjusting the tension of your machine, I highly recommend that you rethread your machine, make sure it is oiled, and make sure the needle is sharp. Oftentimes tension issues can be remedied through these steps.

Packaging Your Quilt

For small quilts and wall hangings you won't need to do what's called packaging your quilt, but for larger projects, such as the picnic blanket on p. 86, you will need to do this.

When you package a quilt, you are rolling it up so that you can focus on quilting one section at a time. Starting at one side, roll your quilt toward the middle, then roll the opposite side until you have what looks like a scroll that has both ends rolled in. Some quilters use clips to secure the rolls, but I do not.

Take your scroll to the machine and position it so that the rolls are on either side of the presser foot area. Leave about a 10-in. section unrolled for quilting. If your quilt is really large, use a table in front of the machine for overflow quilt and use an ironing board behind you to hold the back portion of the quilt.

PART TWO

Patterns & Projects

Lesson 3

NATURE-INSPIRED PATTERNS

This lesson features my take on several quilting motifs that you might find in nature. The simplicity of shapes found in the natural world can be translated into these quilted motifs that create a soft, delicate effect on your quilt. Play around with these designs and their soft curves and wavy patterns and explore designs of your own that could translate into a quilting design. The sky's the limit!

Warmup with Pencil and Paper

For each of the designs in this book, you'll go through a warmup exercise with pencil and paper before you start stitching. This practice allows your body and brain to learn the design and internalize it. The most important guideline for pencil and paper warmups is to not lift your pencil! You will not be able to do this with your quilting, so it is important to practice this. Retrace your lines when you need to in order to travel without lifting your pencil.

With pencil and paper you'll be moving the pencil while the paper stays stationary; with quilting, the opposite happens—your machine is stationary and the quilt top moves. The difference doesn't matter, though. Your body and brain are still learning the design when you practice this way and internalizing the design.

Feel free to practice the designs directly in this book (see the worksheet on p. 32). You can also practice them on a separate sheet of paper (blank or a photocopy of the worksheet page) or in a note-book if you desire.

Getting Ready to Stitch

To help get even more comfortable, I suggest you make a practice quilt sandwich before stitching the design on your finished project. This allows you to focus on practicing the design without worrying about the weight of a bulkier, larger quilt.

It's a great idea to make a few quilt sandwiches at one time, so that you can continue to practice this design or others when you're in the rhythm of stitching. For one quilt sandwich, cut one 13-in. fabric square and one 12-in. fabric square. Cut one 12½-in. square of batting. Layer the fabric and batting: first lay the 13-in. square right side down, then center the batting square on the fabric square, and then place the 12-in. square right side up on top of the batting. Use nine safety pins to baste the corners and quadrants.

PEBBLES

For me, there is no other word to describe this pattern than "zen." Whether it's the sound of a babbling brook that pebbles evoke or the meditative state that making this shape can provoke, I always find myself taken away to a nature when I'm quilting pebbles. This pattern is a favorite of my students.

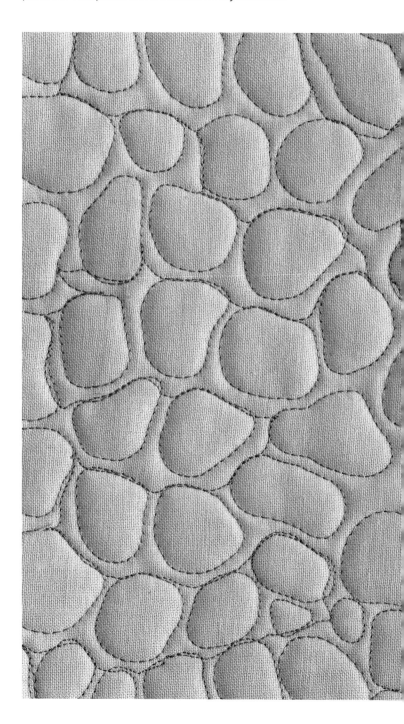

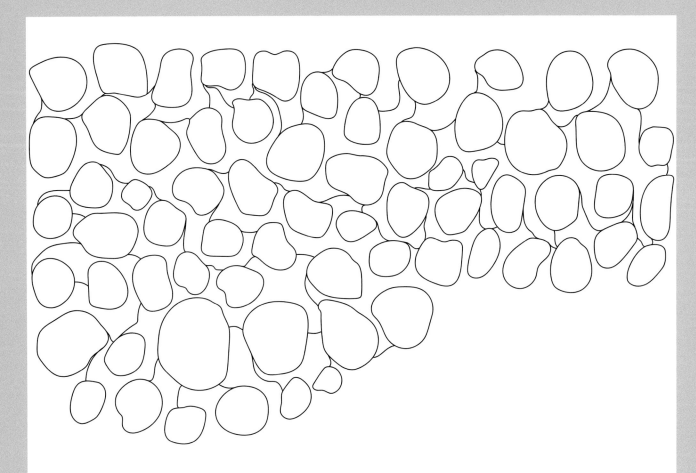

Stitch it

1. This is a "start anywhere" motif, so find a starting point. This could be the corner of a block or the top corner of your quilt or quilted section. For example, if I am making pebbles as an overall motif, I might start at the top left corner. If I am making pebbles in a particular section (i.e., in the middle of a block), then I start anywhere within that block. Begin by making security stitches (see p. 23).

2. Start the first pebble, heading in one direction (I chose counterclockwise). Make sure you complete the entire circumference of your pebble and then stop. Don't forget to keep your machine speed at a steady pace. **(A)**

3. Travel to the next pebble by stitching over one edge of the first pebble until you reach the starting point of the next pebble, connecting the two. **(B)**

4. Stitch the next pebble, making sure you complete the entire shape before moving on. **(C)** Note that you can sew in either direction—clockwise or counterclockwise. Just be consistent in the direction you take.

5. Continue sewing pebbles, stitching over one edge of the pebble just stitched to connect it to another pebble. **(D)** It's easiest to make stacks of two pebbles and then move to the right and make another stack of two pebbles that are offset from the first. **(E)**

6. Continue sewing pebbles over the entire quilt, playing with scale and shape. The space between the pebbles can vary, but be sure each one is connected to the previous pebble. When you reach the last pebble and are ready to stop, end with security stitches.

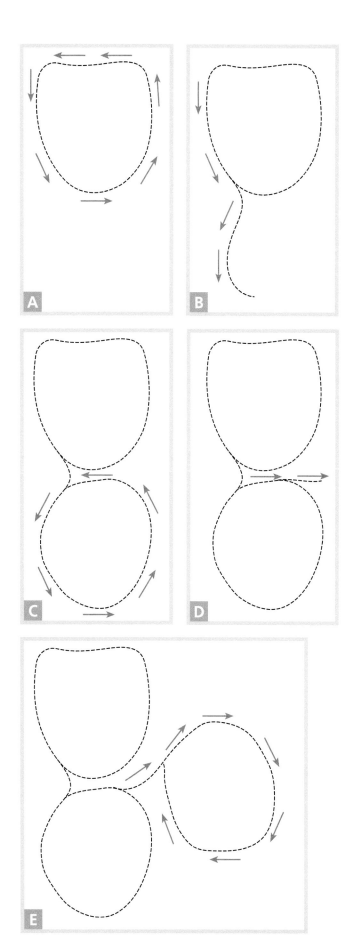

 Design Advice

If you don't complete the entire shape, your pebbles will begin to look more like infinity signs and less round. To avoid this effect, make sure you close the entire circumference of your pebble and then stop before deciding where you'll head for your next shape.

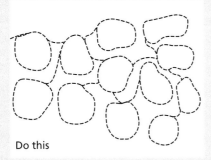

Do this

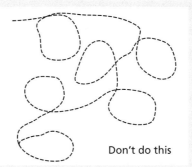

Don't do this

If you are filling a large space with pebbles, make sure you move organically from left to right, then down, as if you're creating rows. Although pebble size and shape should also be organic, the consistency of creating rows will make the quilting pattern unified, as shown in the illustration.

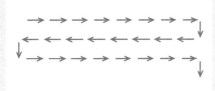

Do this

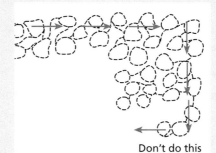

Don't do this

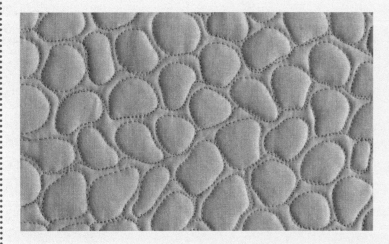

Restitching your lines makes the quilting more bold. If you are using a thread color that contrasts with your backing fabric, keep this in mind. Because I tend to quilt pebbles to fade into the background, I typically use a matching thread color, This is each quilter's artistic choice!

WAVES

This design is reminiscent of the beautiful sedimentary rocks that I see on hikes in the Bay Area and also of desert sand dunes and the ripple effect of raindrops on water. This pattern is a beautiful filler to create texture in a border or in a pieced area of your quilt. (Practice on the worksheet on p. 36.)

On a regular sewing machine, the horizontal stitching area for this design will be limited—about 10 in. across is comfortable. I encourage you to practice on a column of space that is only about 4 in. wide, however. On a longarm, you can create this wave pattern from left to right on an entire quilt top.

Stitch it

1. Determine your columns, or boundary lines. These can either be marked on your quilt top with your marking pencil or they can be established by seam lines or the fabric design of the pieced quilt top. See my note above about width of surface area.

2. Pick a starting point on the left boundary line and make security stitches.

3. Begin sewing a straightish line from left to right, ending on the right boundary line. **(A)**

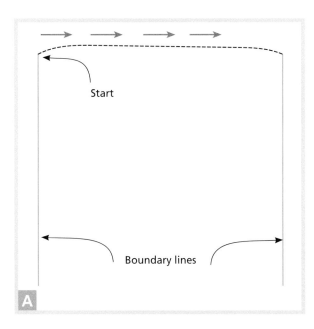

TRACE AND PRACTICE

4. To turn back, stitch down the boundary line a few stitches (the number of stitches can vary, but three to four is a good number) before you begin sewing from right to left. **(B)**

5. Stitch back to the left boundary line. You can follow the previous line's shape or vary it in order to create texture. Remember, like nature, the lines can be organic and not perfectly straight. **(C)**

6. Repeat step 4, stitching down a few stitches, and then stitch a line to the right again, ending at the boundary line.

7. Continue in this way to complete the quilting pattern, ending with security stitches. **(D)**

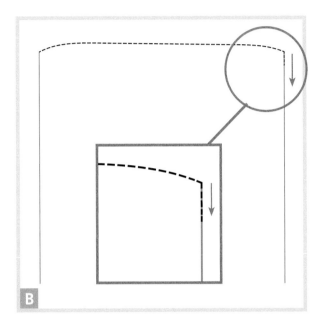

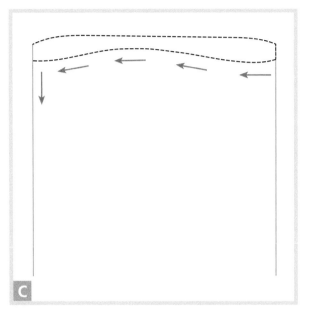

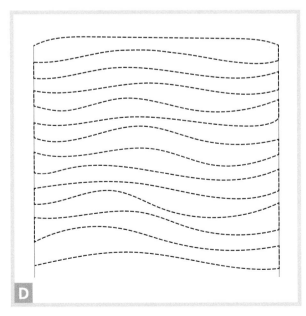

Design Advice

You can alter the look of whatever you're quilting by adding details to the quilting pattern or combining patterns.

- Vary the wave height gradually. Play around with big vertical upward waves, and then even them out into straighter waves. Leave bigger spaces between lines or tighten the space between lines to create different effects.

- Play around with a few variations on this design. You can add texture by creating what looks like a tree knot. **(A)**

- Break up the waves by stopping halfway into a wave line, repositioning the quilt, and stitching back the way you just came, adding visual movement. **(B)**

- Combine quilting patterns in your quilt top. If you're not inspired to use different quilting patterns, let the patchwork piecing be your guide. Here, a portion of a half-square triangle has a different pattern to highlight the fabric. Waves fill the rest of the block. **(C)**

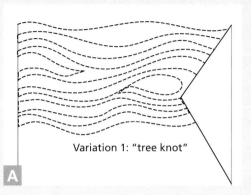

Variation 1: "tree knot"

A

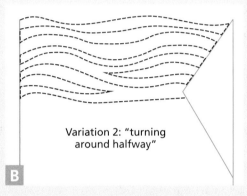

Variation 2: "turning around halfway"

B

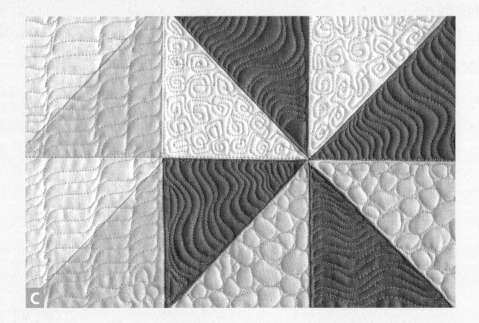

C

WHALE TAILS

This is one of the more structured designs in my collection, making it perfect for a border or rectangular area where you are looking for a more intentional pattern. The central part of this pattern is a horizontal line; the beginning flares down and the end flares up (or vice versa depending on which column of stitching you're working on). The overall motif that comes out of repeating this shape in a columnar area evokes the imagery of a beautiful humpback whale breaching and flashing her tail.

For the best results with this design, work in columns that are 2 in. to 2½ in. wide. As with the other designs, trace and practice right in this book before stitching. See the template on p. 40.

Stitch it

1. Measure across the entire width of the quilt top you're quilting, then divide that total by 2 or 2½. With a marking pencil, mark boundary lines and then columns that are all the same width for consistency in the quilting pattern. **(A)**

2. Start at the top of the left column and make security stitches (see p. 23). Remember that the first part of the pattern flares up.

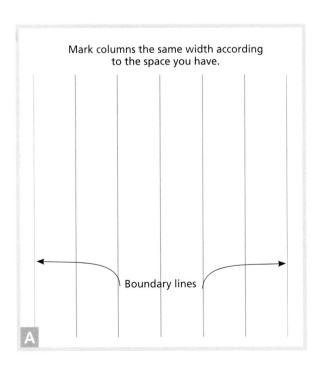

Mark columns the same width according to the space you have.

Boundary lines

A

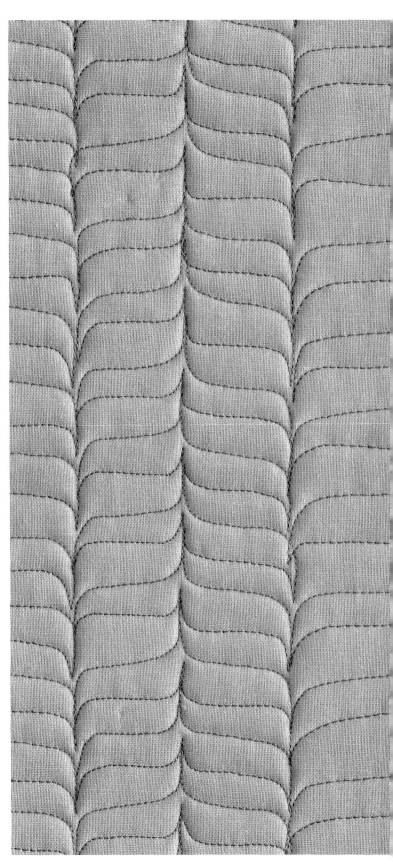

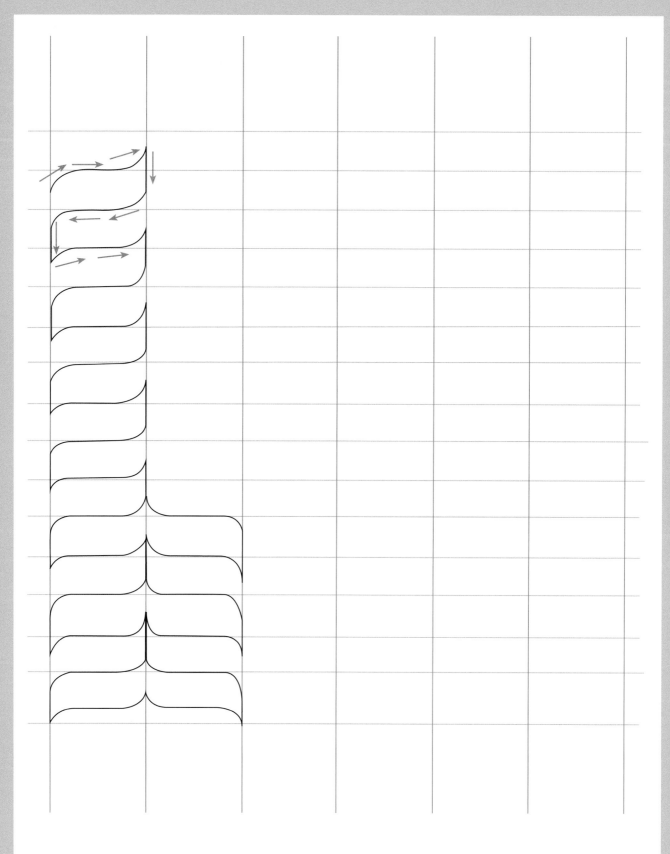

3. Begin quilting a line from left to right, according to the illustration, flaring the end of the pattern up. **(B)**

4. To turn back, stitch down the boundary line of the column; the number of stitches varies, but three or four stitches are good. Then stitch from right to left, completing the shape; follow the first stitching line as a guide for consistency in shape. **(C)** In the whale tail design it is best to keep the number of stitches between quilting lines consistent so that the shape is uniform across the quilt.

5. Continue quilting down the left column, stitching from left to right, then turning back to stitch from right to left. **(D)**

6. When you've reached the bottom of the left column, start stitching the right column, working from the bottom up to the top of the quilt and mirroring the design of the left column. **(E)**

7. Continue quilting whale tails in columns across the quilt top, ending with security stitches.

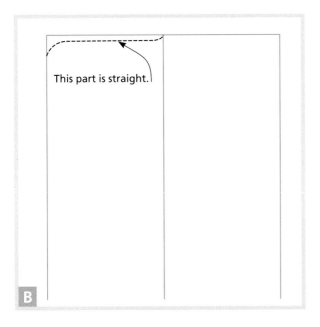

This part is straight.

B

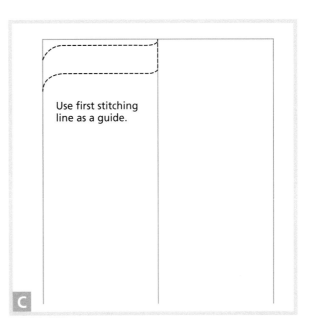

Use first stitching line as a guide.

C

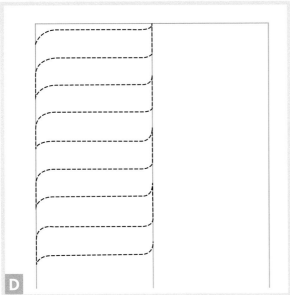

D

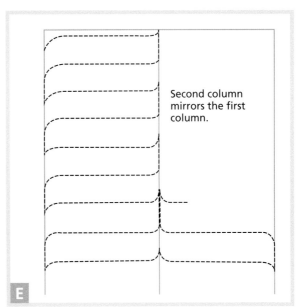

Second column mirrors the first column.

E

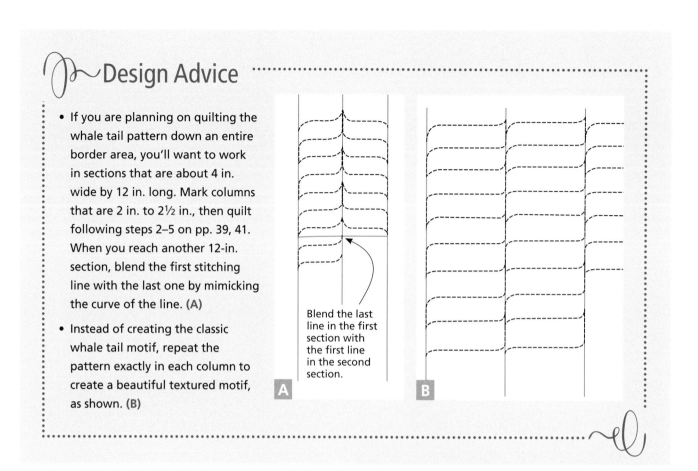

Design Advice

- If you are planning on quilting the whale tail pattern down an entire border area, you'll want to work in sections that are about 4 in. wide by 12 in. long. Mark columns that are 2 in. to 2½ in., then quilt following steps 2–5 on pp. 39, 41. When you reach another 12-in. section, blend the first stitching line with the last one by mimicking the curve of the line. **(A)**

- Instead of creating the classic whale tail motif, repeat the pattern exactly in each column to create a beautiful textured motif, as shown. **(B)**

Blend the last line in the first section with the first line in the second section.

A

B

LEAVES

I grew up in the Midwest, and raking leaves in the fall stands out in my memory. Now that I live in California, my connection to leaves has changed. One of my favorite things to do is explore one of the many botanical gardens in my area. Time passes by quickly when I get lost in the stunning array of trees and plants from all over the world, from New Zealand to Chile.

No matter where we live, one natural phenomenon we all have in common is the simple beauty of leaves. This quilting motif is designed to inspire you to observe your own environment and find leaf shapes that are unique to your area.

This is a "start anywhere" motif, so find your own starting point. This could be the corner of a block or the top corner of your quilt or quilted section. For example, if I am making leaves as an overall motif, I might start at the top left corner. If I am making leaves in a particular section (i.e., in the middle of a block), then I'll start anywhere within that block. Leaves will be connected together with "chains."

Stitch it

1. Begin your first leaf by making security stitches (see p. 23).

2. Start a leaf chain first with the stem, then with the left side of the leaf, which is basically a curved line; the illustration shows a cutout in the line, to mimic an actual leaf, but feel free to eliminate that from your design. **(A)**

3. When you reach the tip of the leaf, pivot the quilt top and then stitch the right side of the leaf. **(B)**

4. Once you reach the bottom of the leaf, finish it by stitching a stem spine up through the middle. **(C)**

5. Continue up through the tip of the leaf to connect the completed leaf to the next one. Make another leaf following steps 2-4. **(D)** If you are making leaves in a column, sew a connecting line to continue up or down.

6. Continue quilting leaf chains until the quilt top is complete. End with security stitches.

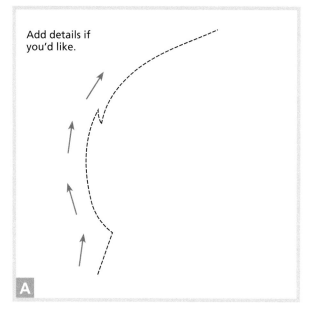

Add details if you'd like.

A

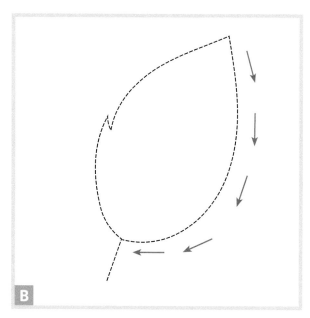

B

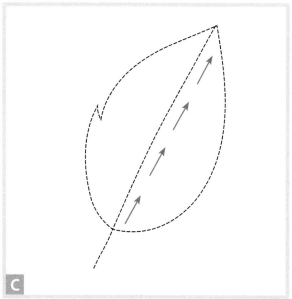

C

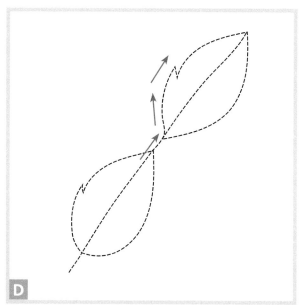

D

Instead of making a leaf chain, create bunches of leaves by retracing the middle spine to return to your starting point.

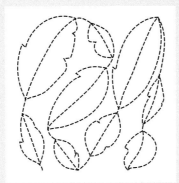

Play with the scale and shape of the leaves, making some big or small, wide or narrow in order to fill space and to create visual texture.

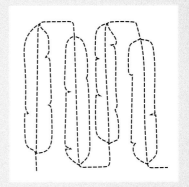

Alter the leaf shape to make feathers by elongating the basic shape.

DAISIES

This motif is one of the most fun for me not only because it reminds me of the 1970s "flower power" slogan, but also because I love the versatility of this simple flower design. The design is also a favorite of my students! Ideal for a baby quilt or a picnic blanket, this daisy pattern can cover an entire quilt top or can be used as a background filler for a pieced section of a quilt. (Practice on the worksheet on p. 46.)

Stitch it

1. This is a "start anywhere" motif, so find a starting point. For beginners, I would encourage you to start at the corner of a block or the top corner of your quilt. Begin your first daisy by making security stitches.

2. Start the daisy chain by making a stem. Length can vary, but it should be at least 1 in. long. **(A, p. 47)**

3. Create the center disk by stitching a circle, following the direction of the arrows in the illustration. **(B, p. 47)**

4. Now begin creating the petals, starting and ending each petal where it meets the circle. I recommend making five petals that are about the same size for each daisy. Once you've completed the first petal, you'll need to pivot your quilt to start the second one. **(C)**

5. Continue stitching petals. You should end the final petal where you started—where the stem and the first petal join the circle. **(D)**

6. Make the next stem. You will need to trace a portion of the center disk until you reach the place where you want to stitch a new daisy. Take a few stitches for the stem, then stitch the next center disk. **(E)**

7. Continue with steps 3–6 to complete the quilting. When you are finished, end with security stitches.

 Design Advice

Play with the scale of the daisies for texture and variety. Because the petals can be different sizes, smaller daisies can nicely fill holes between larger ones.

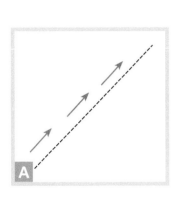

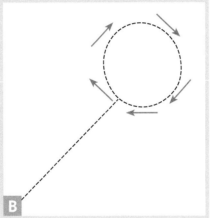

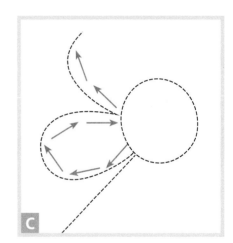

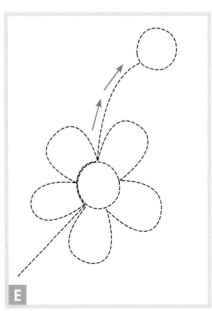

Rustic Placemats

Nothing completes a dining table setting quite like placemats. This project is an ideal way to show off your free-motion quilting and will give you an excuse to invite some friends over for a meal. The zigzag finish on these placemats gives them a rustic quality, and they're sure to give your place settings a personal touch. What's more, they are reversible, so you can play around with different combinations for your table.

For these placemats, I like to use a linen/cotton blend for a more earthy texture. For a thicker, heavier loft, I use a 100% cotton batting; for a lighter, more airy loft, use a cotton/polyester blend.

You will trim the edges of the placemat top about ¼ in. after quilting so keep that in mind as you position your design.

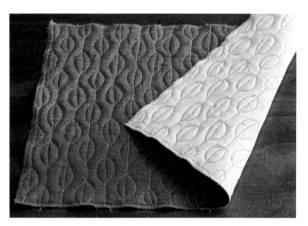

MATERIALS AND SUPPLIES

For one placemat:

- One 12½-in. by 18½-in. rectangle of top fabric
- One 13-in. by 19-in. rectangle of batting
- One 13½-in. by 19½-in. rectangle of backing fabric
- Thread of choice
- Hand-sewing needle
- Safety pins for basting
- Sewing machine attachments: regular foot for zigzag stitch and darning foot for free-motion quilting

Make the Placemats

1. Form a quilt sandwich. Place the backing fabric right side down, position the batting over the backing, and then position the top fabric right side up over the batting. Baste the quilt sandwich with pins. **(A)**

2. Hand-baste to secure the edges. **(B)**

3. Choose your favorite quilting motif and quilt the placemat top, removing the safety pins as needed. **(C)**

4. Once the placemat is filled with quilting, block the edges: Trim ¼ in. from all edges of the top fabric. This will also trim off all excess backing and batting, as well as square up your placemat to an even 12-in. by 18-in. rectangle. **(D)**

5. Using a tight zigzag stitch—around a 1 on the stitch length dial—stitch around the perimeter of your placemat to finish the edge (see the photos on the facing page). If you'd prefer, add binding on your placemat instead (see p. 96).

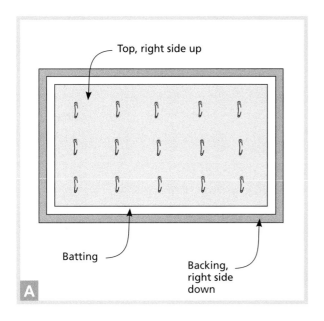

Top, right side up

Batting

Backing, right side down

A

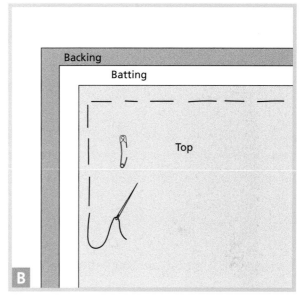

Backing

Batting

Top

B

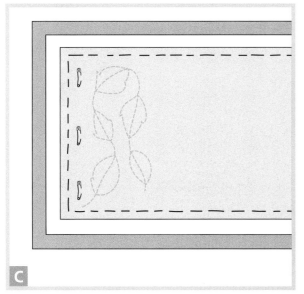

C

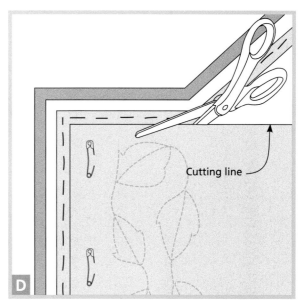

Cutting line

D

Lesson 4

GEOMETRIC PATTERNS

Nothing says modern quite like straight lines, minimalism, and crisp, clean angles. These geometric designs are the antithesis of the decorative nature patterns in the previous lesson, but they just might be the perfect complement to your quilt top. Try these patterns on their own for a more linear, angular effect or in combination with some leaves or waves to create a more embellished overall motif.

A reminder that approximately ¼ in. of your quilt top will be covered by binding.

Warmup

As with Lesson 3, each design in this lesson starts with a warmup exercise using pencil and paper. Follow the practice pages as many times as needed, and work hard to keep your pencil on paper. Practice traveling between shapes, too. Most importantly, remember that getting good at free-motion quilting takes practice. Start by tracing the designs directly in this book, then move to a separate piece of paper, and then take the leap and move to your sewing machine.

See pp. 20–21 to make a quilt sandwich—or two or three!—to practice stitching on before jumping into your quilt. If you like the way the quilt sandwich looks, then start free-motion stitching your quilt. If not, practice on another quilt sandwich until you are comfortable with the design.

GEOMETRIC SWIRLS

This is my favorite free-motion warmup pattern, and it makes a beautiful background filler for any modern quilt. Consider this a modern take on the stippling motif that you sometimes see in more traditional quilts. (Practice on the worksheet on p. 52.)

Stitch it

1. This is a "start anywhere" motif, so find a starting point and begin by making your security stitches (see p. 23).

2. Move into your first swirl. I make the outer soft-cornered square first and work in a counterclockwise direction. **(A)** You can stitch in either a clockwise or counterclockwise direction; just follow the same direction throughout stitching the swirls. **(B)**

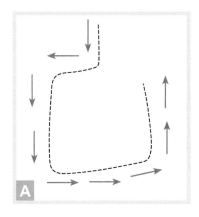

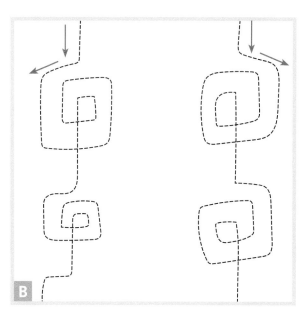

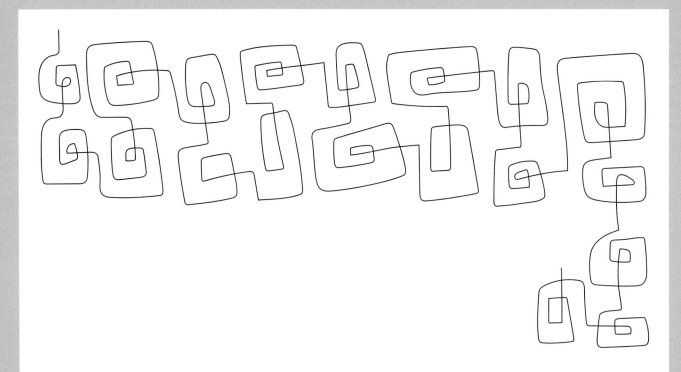

3. Begin to swirl inside the soft-corner square, making one or two inner shapes. **(C)**

4. At the center point of the soft-corner square, travel to the next swirl by stitching a straight line through the swirl in either direction. **(D)**

5. Continue sewing swirls over the entire quilt. When you reach the end of the last swirl, finish with security stitches.

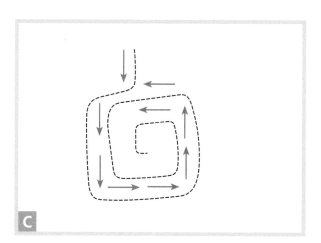

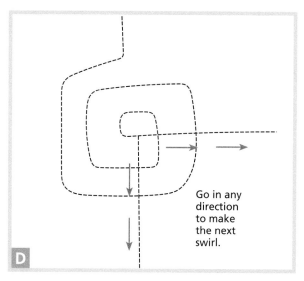

Go in any direction to make the next swirl.

~Design Advice

- Move across your quilt top or quilted area from left to right, then down, then right to left. This creates a nice flow and reduces the number of times you need to stop to cut threads and start again. Vary the size of your swirls and number of inner shapes in each to help blend the rows of stitching together.

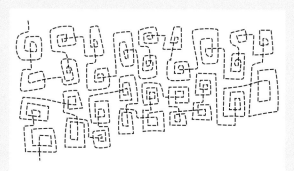

- As you stitch, you might find yourself creating soft-corner squares, hard-angle squares, or even circles. That's okay. Let the design be fluid and have fun with it.

WONKY HEXAGONS

A hexagon is any six-sided shape. Nuts and bolts, the design of a soccer ball, honeycombs, and a tortoise shell all have a hexagon as part of their design. Shapes that are less regular create a more interesting quilting design than if the shapes are identical. But while the length and position of each side of the shape can vary, as long as the shape has six sides, you can't go wrong.

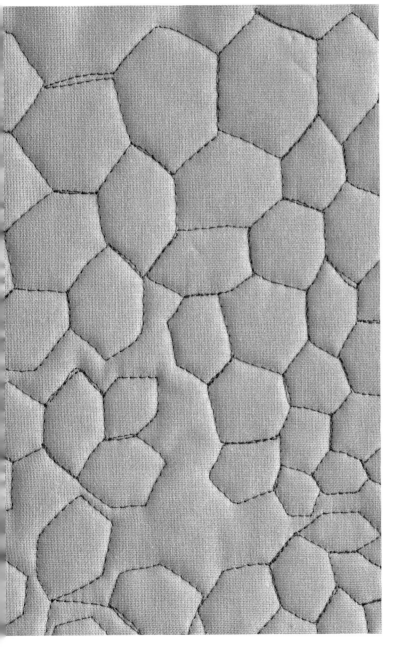

Stitch it

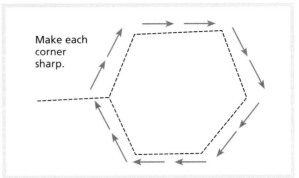

Make each corner sharp.

1. This is a "start anywhere" motif, so find a starting point and begin by making security stitches.

2. Create your first hexagon. Pause at each corner to make sure it is sharp before continuing stitching to the next corner. You don't want a soft-cornered hexagon, which is essentially just a circle!

3. At this point, you have two design options: The first is to cluster your hexagons together to create a consistent and fuller design. The second is to connect individual hexagons with a straight line to create a new hexagon that shares no sides with any other.

DESIGN OPTION: CLUSTERED HEXAGONS

1. Create a second hexagon that has one side in common with the first one. You will need to retrace one side at least to do so. (A)

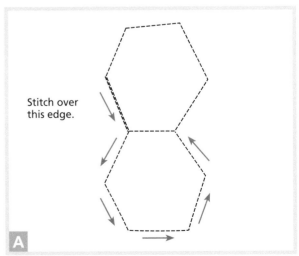

Stitch over this edge.

A

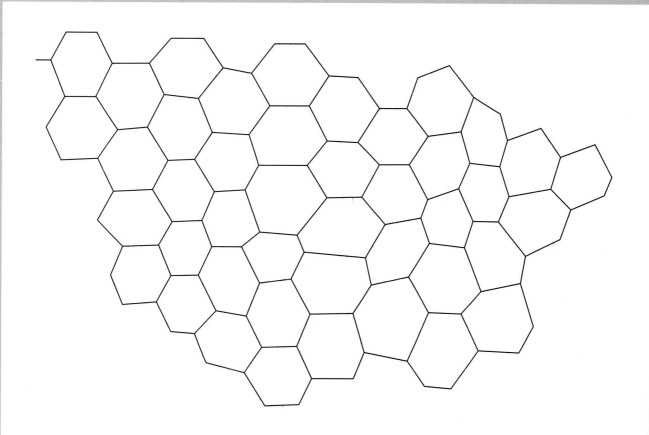

2. Stitch another hexagon, which might share two sides with other hexagons. **(B)**

3. Continue the pattern, creating a wonky hexagon design over the entire quilt—vary the size of hexagons but keep them clustered. This will form what I call a wonky honeycomb. **(C)** End with security stitches.

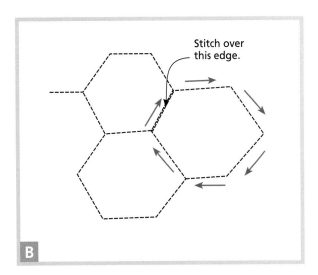

Stitch over this edge.

B

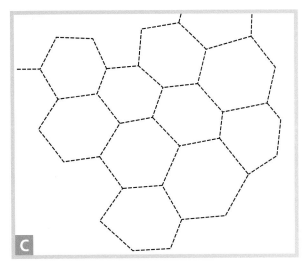

C

TIP Be sure to practice this pattern with pencil and paper until the six-sided shape becomes more natural.

 Design Advice

- Play with the scale of the hexagons to create interest.

- If you choose to cluster hexagons, you will need to retrace at least one side of each hexagon. If you are using a thread color that contrasts with your backing fabric, be aware that retracing your lines will make the quilting bolder.

- Similar to pebbles, this is a nice motif to create background texture as opposed to a visible design. If subtle texture is your intention, use a thread color that matches your fabric and the quilting will fade into the background nicely.

DESIGN OPTION: INDIVIDUAL HEXAGONS

1. Stitch a straight line into an open space and then create another hexagon.

2. Continue in this manner, connecting hexagons with straight lines, until the entire quilt top is quilted. **(A)** End with security stitches.

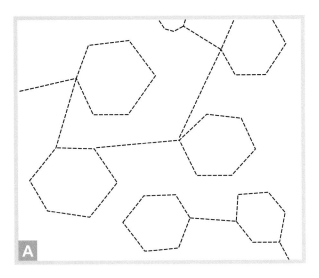

A

FOUR-POINTED STARS

This motif is reminiscent of the traditional orange-peel quilt design, but stylistically, there are many ways to interpret it. My inspiration for this motif comes from the design of an iron gate in my neighborhood (see the bottom photo on p. 5). Usually when I quilt this design, however, the four-pointed stars morph from a rigid grid to a more free-form motif. I've included design options for both. Play around to discover what you like best.

Students in my quilting classes love this design because there are so many design options. (Practice on the worksheet on p. 58.)

Stitch it

DESIGN OPTION: GRIDDED STARS

1. Determine the size of your grid and use a marking pencil to transfer it to your quilt top. Include only one star per square. **(A)**

2. Start at the top left square, and begin by making security stitches. Following the illustration, stitch the top of each star in each square in row 1. **(B)**

3. When you get to the star on the far right (star 4 in the illustration), stitch the right side of that star and then complete the bottom and left side of star 4. Be sure the corners are sharp. **(C)**

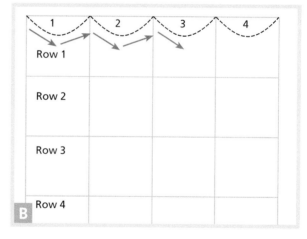

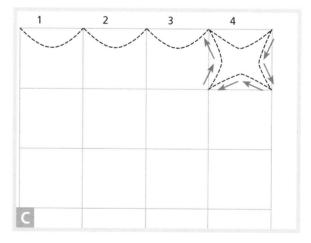

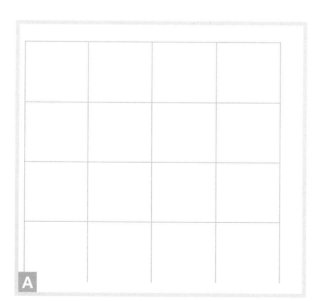

4. Complete star 3 by stitching down the right, bottom, and left sides, as shown. **(D)**

5. Repeat to stitch stars 2 and 1 in row 1.

6. When star 1 in row 1 is complete, restitch the left side of star 1 so that you end up at the top of star 1 in row 2. **(E)]**

7. Repeat steps 2–6 to complete the quilt top. End with security stitches.

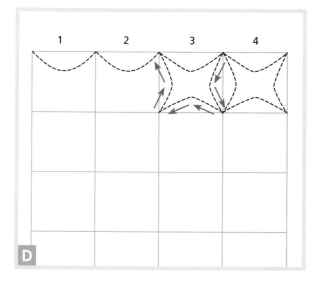

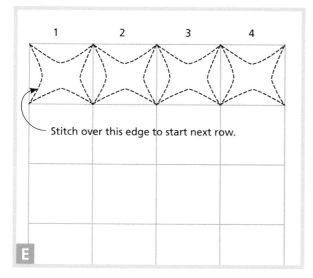

Stitch over this edge to start next row.

TIP If you are creating a gridded star design, I highly encourage you to practice a lot with pencil and paper before quilting to get comfortable with working in a grid. Be sure to mark out the grid on your quilt top using a marking pencil and ruler.

DESIGN OPTION: FREE-FORM STARS

As with other designs, vary the size of the stars if you like. This gives your design more texture.

1. This is a "start anywhere" motif, so find a starting point and begin by making security stitches.

2. Create a four-pointed star, moving from your starting point in either a clockwise or counterclockwise direction. As with gridded stars, be sure the corners are crisp. **(A)**

3. Travel to a new starting point by either tracing one side of the star to join the points or stitching a straight line to create a stem between stars. As shown in the illustration, you can also stitch a combination of stars joined at the points or with a stem. **(B)**

4. Begin the next star, following steps 2–3, then continue stitching stars until you have filled the quilt top. Don't forget to end with security stitches.

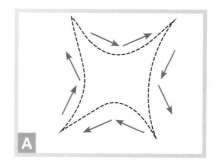

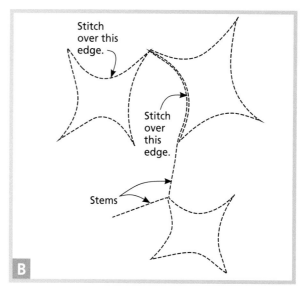

Stitch over this edge.

Stitch over this edge.

Stems

TRAVELING SPIRALS

Did you or your kids ever play with a Spirograph? I have fond memories of using bright colors and cranking around those wheels to create loopy and beautiful spiral stars. These traveling blobs are inspired by those shapes and are designed to create a beautiful wandering spiral pattern for your quilts.

This design is one of the simplest since spirals flow from one to the next, and adding variety in size and shape is encouraged. This means whatever goes!

Stitch it

1. This is a "start anywhere" motif, so find a starting point and begin by making security stitches.

2. My first spiral is an oval shape, but yours can be more circular. **(A)**

3. As you get close to where you started, continue making a similar spiral that is positioned slightly downward. You will not trace over stitches already made. **(B)**

4. As with the first spiral, when you get close to where you started on the second spiral, form another spiral shape from the previous one. Make sure each one is "traveling" in a different direction than the

one before. This will ensure that your quilting is evenly distributed. **(C)**

5. Continue until the entire quilt top is quilted. **(D)**

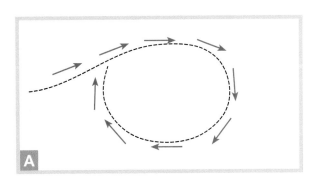

A

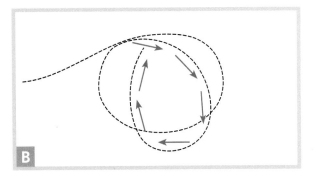

B

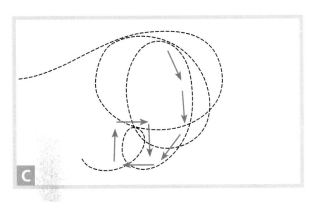

C

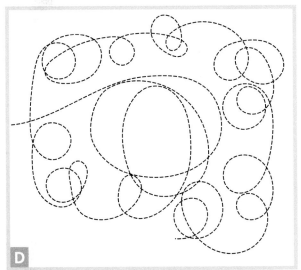

D

TRIANGLES

Oh, how I LOVE triangles! I'm not sure when or why my love affair with triangles began, but this shape, whether I'm doodling it on paper or quilting it into a quilt or handbag, makes me so happy.

I've provided two design options here. The first is a random, free-form triangle motif where you can play around with shape, scale, and patterning. The second is more structured, where you create lines of triangle chains, reminiscent of vertical window blinds. Both are wonderful for any project at any scale. (Practice on the worksheet on p. 64.)

Stitch it

DESIGN OPTION: RANDOM TRIANGLES

1. This is a "start anywhere" motif, so find a starting point and begin by making security stitches.

2. Make your first triangle. Similar to the hexagons, make sure the corners are sharp in order to make a triangle shape, not a bean or an oval.

3. To make the next triangle, either begin directly at the point of your first one, connecting the two, or travel to a new area with a straight line, leaving space between shapes. **(A)**

4. Repeat until the entire quilt top is quilted, playing around with placement, scale, and shape of the triangles. **(B)** End with security stitches.

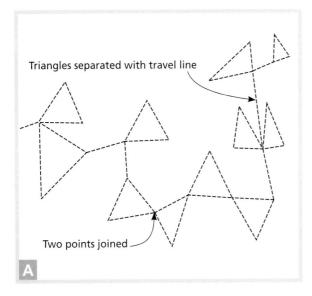

Triangles separated with travel line

Two points joined

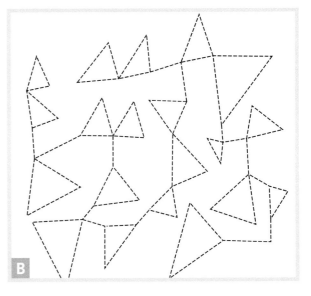

DESIGN OPTION: TRIANGLE CHAINS

1. This pattern is stitched from top to bottom of a specific area of your quilt. (You can also start at the bottom and work your way up.)

2. Find a starting point at the top edge and begin by making security stitches.

3. Stitch down in a straight line for about an inch and then make your first triangle, creating first the left side, then the bottom, and then the right side as you stitch back to the starting point. **(A)**

4. To make the next triangle, stitch a line straight down through the center of the triangle, cutting it in half, until you are ready to create your next triangle. I like to leave about the same-length stitching line between triangles, but you can vary it if you'd prefer. **(B)**

5. Repeat until the quilt top is filled and end stitching with security stitches.

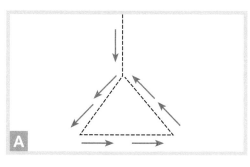

A

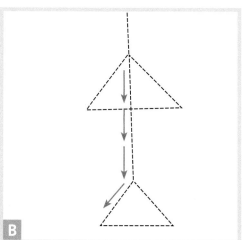

B

 Design Advice

On a smaller quilt, work down one column and then up the next until the top is quilted. For a larger quilt, I recommend you start at the same edge of your quilt for each column, so you'll need to stop at the bottom of each column with a straight line and security stitches, cut your threads, and then start again at the top of a new column.

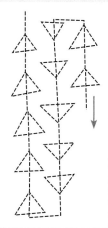

Stitch over this edge.

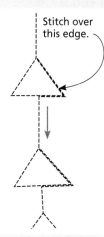

If you're making triangle chains and would rather not cut your triangle in half with a stitching line, you can retrace one side and half of the bottom before stitching a new straight line. Note that this tracing will make these parts of the triangle bold from double stitching.

For both design options, play with placement, shape, scale, and direction! Also, consider echo-quilting or outline-quilting some or all of the triangles for added interest.

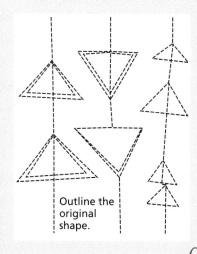

Outline the original shape.

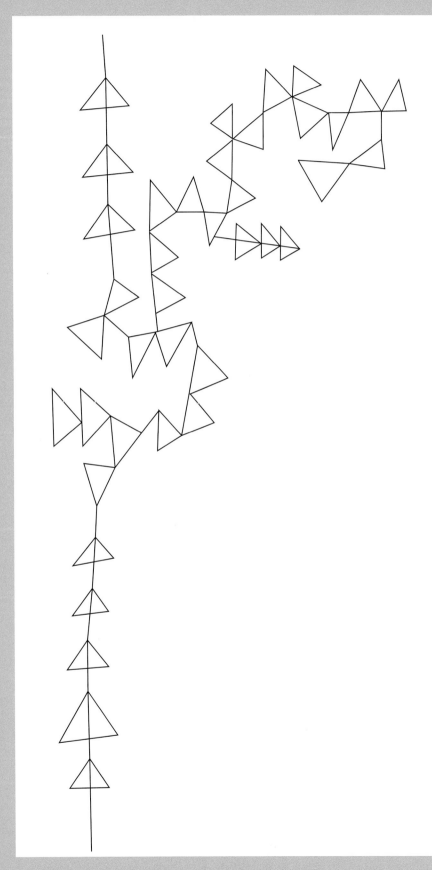

Quilted Tote Bag

Can I tell you a little secret? This tote bag is one of my favorite projects. It combines two of my biggest crafting loves: quilting and bag making. With boxed corners and a leather strap, this is not your typical quilted tote bag. It is extremely versatile and useful, and it is a fun and stylish way to show off your new quilting skills!

MATERIALS AND SUPPLIES

- Two 15-in. by 16-in. rectangles of cotton or linen fabric for the top
- Two 15½-in. by 16½-in. rectangles of batting (I prefer a cotton/poly blend)
- Two 16-in. by 17-in. rectangles of cotton or linen fabric for the lining
- 2 small scraps of top or lining fabric for attaching the straps, approximately 3½ in. by 12 in.
- 1 leather bag strap (approximately 21 in. long)
- Two 12-in. lengths of ½-in.-wide double-fold bias tape
- Thread of choice
- Safety pins for basting
- Hand-sewing needle
- Sewing machine attachments: darning foot and regular foot
- 2 D-rings or other hardware for attaching the bag strap

Quilt the Bag

1. Make two quilt sandwiches. Place the two rectangles of lining fabric right side down, center the batting over the lining, and then center the top fabric right side up over the batting.

2. Pin-baste the quilt sandwiches all over, then hand-baste the outer edge of each (see p. 20). **(A)**

3. Orient the sandwiches so that one of the shorter sides will be the top of the bag. You can mark the top with a piece of painter's tape to remind yourself. If you are choosing a "start anywhere" motif, you don't need to worry about indicating the top. **(B)**

4. Quilt each sandwich until evenly quilted.

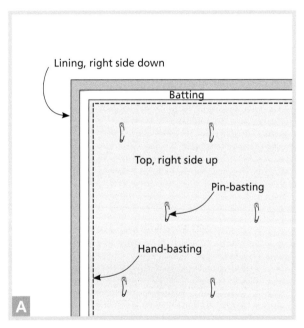

Lining, right side down

Batting

Top, right side up

Pin-basting

Hand-basting

A

Quilt with short side on top.

B

TIP A ⅜-in. seam allowance is usually made by following the edge of your machine's regular foot. Check your machine's instruction manual to be sure this is true for your machine.

Make the Tote

5. Trim away approximately ¼ in. of the batting on each sandwich until it is flush with the top fabric. Do not trim the lining fabric! **(C)**

6. Finish the top edge of both quilt sandwiches by making a double-fold hem. Fold the lining fabric over onto itself ½ in., then press. Fold it over again another ½ in., then press, pin, and stitch. **(D)**

7. Now sew the quilt sandwiches together with a French seam. Position the rectangles so the lining fabrics are facing each other and the edges you just finished are at the top. Pin. Sew a ¼-in. seam around the remaining sides. **(E)**

8. Turn the bag wrong side out so that the quilted "right" sides are facing each other on the inside of the bag. **(F)**

9. Sew a ⅜-in. seam along the same three sides, leaving the top open.

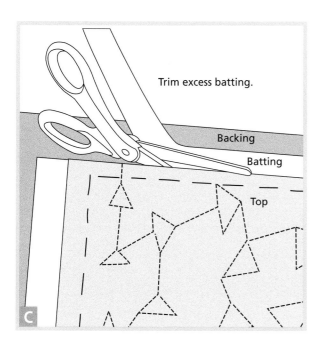

Trim excess batting.

Backing

Batting

Top

C

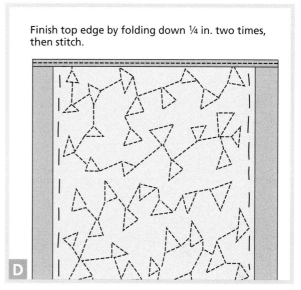

Finish top edge by folding down ¼ in. two times, then stitch.

D

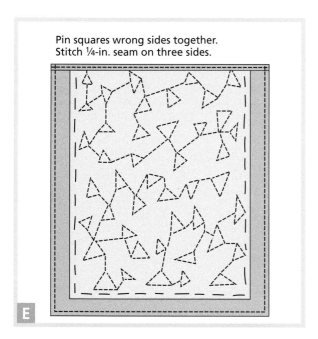

Pin squares wrong sides together. Stitch ¼-in. seam on three sides.

E

Turn wrong side out, then sew ⅜-in. seam on three sides.

F

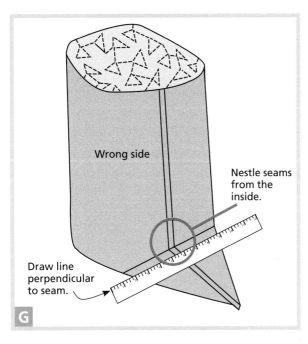

Wrong side

Nestle seams from the inside.

Draw line perpendicular to seam.

G

Box the Corners

10. Give the tote a flat bottom by boxing the corners. With the bag wrong side out, center one corner in the bottom seam and nestle the seams from the inside to smooth them out. A knitting needle or chopstick works well here. Then use a ruler to draw a line that is 7¼ in. long from edge to edge. **(G)**

11. Sew along this line, and then cut off the remaining triangle, leaving a ¼-in. seam allowance. **(H)** Repeat on the other side.

12. Hide the raw edges by attaching a piece of ½-in.-wide double-fold bias tape with a straight stitch. **(I)**

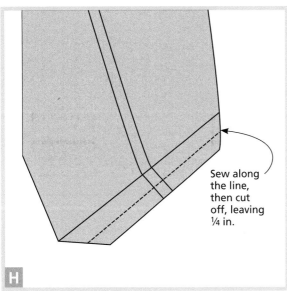

Sew along the line, then cut off, leaving ¼ in.

H

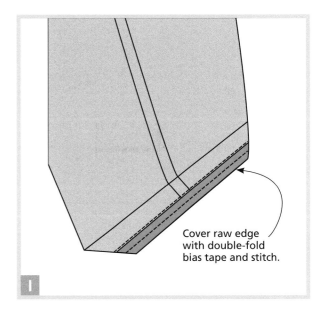

Cover raw edge with double-fold bias tape and stitch.

I

Attach the Bag Handles

Note: These instructions are specific to the type of strap I used that has two 1-in. D-ring attachments.

13. Create bias tape from a scrap of top or lining fabric that measures 3½ in. by 12 in. Fold both long sides into the middle so they meet, then fold again. Press and stitch along both sides. **(J)**

Cut the strip in half so that you have two 6-in.-long strips for attaching the strap.

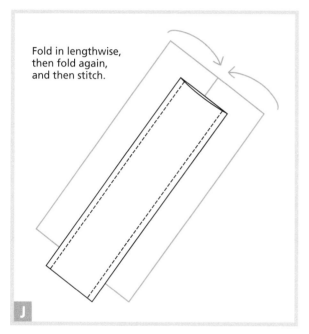

Fold in lengthwise, then fold again, and then stitch.

J

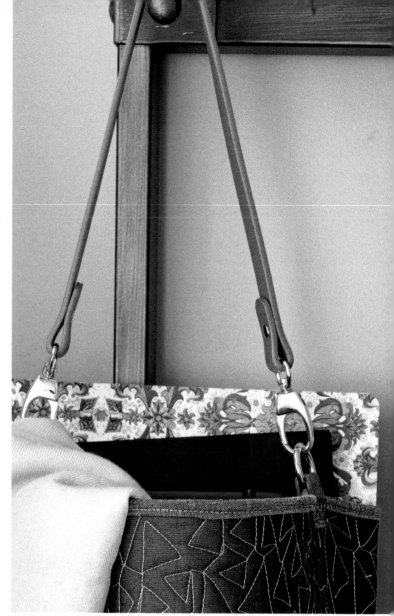

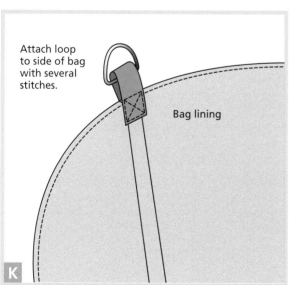

Attach loop to side of bag with several stitches.

Bag lining

K

14. I attached one edge of both strips to the inside of the bag where the top edge seams meet, reinforcing it with several backstitches and a stitched X. **(K)**

15. I slipped a D-ring on each strip, then folded over and stitched the other edge of the strips to the bag with backstitches and an X. Then I attached the leather bag strip to the D rings.

Lesson 5

MIXED-MEDIA DESIGNS

Consider this lesson your intro to simple collage quilting, with designs that involve painting on fabric and stitching around the painting, appliqué, and block lettering. As with the patterns in the other lessons, practice these straightforward exercises on both paper and practice quilt sandwiches before moving on to creating your own layered mixed-media quilting designs. Remember that binding will cover ¼ in. around the edges of your quilt top, so plan your design accordingly.

Painting on Fabric and Free-Motion Quilting around It

This is my favorite free-motion quilting design hands down, and it came about after I took an introductory watercolor painting course that triggered an instantaneous obsession with watercolor painting. I painted mostly abstract blobs and circles, experimenting with blending and bleeding. After my designs dried, I outlined the edges with a thin black marker, which looked a lot like quilting. This led me to combine textile painting with free-form stitching to create a quilt top with a watercolor effect.

Unlike the other lessons in this book, there is no workbook page of a pattern to trace and practice since the pattern will follow the edges of the design you paint on fabric. We'll start with painting to create a watercolor style and then quilting around the edges. You can also add one of the quilting patterns from Lessons 3 and 4 to the background of your painting.

BEFORE YOU PAINT
Choosing paint

There is nothing quite like the richness of watercolor paint on a pad of thick, creamy white paper. When I set out to re-create this effect on fabric, my goal was to find a paint that would imitate not only the richness of pigment but also the watery, fluid nature of the paint.

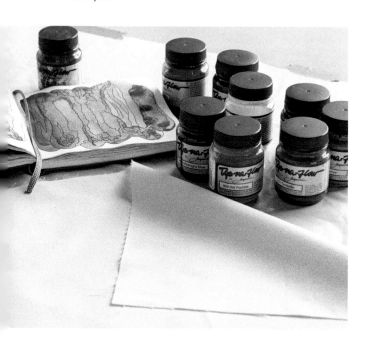

I found both of these qualities in Jacquard's Dye-Na-Flow paint. Considered a liquid acrylic paint, Dye-Na-Flow comes in 32 different colors, some of them extremely saturated and vibrant, others muted and natural. When heat-set, this paint is permanent on textiles, making it perfect even for fabric that you will wash and use every day.

Due to its liquid consistency, Dye-Na-Flow works just like watercolor paint, even straight from the bottle. However, depending on the effect you desire, adding water can increase transparency or dilute the pigment, just as with watercolor on paper.

Choosing fabric type and color

In addition to searching for the perfect paint, I also set out to find the best fabric to re-create the cold-press paper effect. I learned there are many options.

Fabrics that are PFD, or "prepared for dye," hold the paint spectacularly since they are designed to receive pigment. However, paint on this type of fabric bleeds extensively, which means that you don't have as much precision if you are painting delicate lines or details. In my experience, most "white" fabrics, whether they are PFD or not, react to paint in this same way. This includes Robert Kaufman's Kona solids such as Snow and Ivory.

Natural cotton fabrics, on the other hand, are not bleached and do not absorb paints or dyes as quickly or intensely as PFD fabrics. This means that fabrics made with natural fibers will allow your painted line to have a crisp "edge." For an effect most similar to that of watercolor paint on cold-press watercolor paper, natural is the way to go. Natural cottons that create this effect include most natural muslins or the Kona color Natural, which is my preferred fabric. These fabrics often have a speckled look and appear to have slight texture. A potential downside to these fabrics is that they have a slightly off-white color.

Muslin fabrics allow a sharp, crisp edge to your painted designs but are markedly thinner than quilting cottons. This means they are not as durable and are more translucent than quilting cottons. Why is this important? If you are making a quilt that will be used or washed, the fibers of thin muslins will not last as long as quilting cotton. Also, you are more likely to see through to the backing fabric. Quilting cottons will also allow your painted designs to have a crisp edge. They are less see-through and more durable than muslin, and they are most likely to withstand heavy use.

Fabric color is personal choice. All fabrics have different dye lots, which have slightly different shades. Keep this in mind if you are making a quilt that requires multiple yards of fabric.

MATERIALS AND SUPPLIES

No matter what design you are painting, you'll need the following supplies in addition to paint and fabric:

- A variety of paintbrushes: 1-in. brushes for thicker lines, finer brushes for detail work
- A palette for mixing; an ice cube tray works great for this purpose!
- Jars of water: I use two—one for warm colors, one for cool colors
- Paper towels for blotting
- A surface for painting: I lay down drop cloths on my table and floors (Dye-Na-Flow can stain your carpet, tile, and wood floors)

TECHNIQUES FOR PAINTING
Thick brush: Large downward-sweeping action

Perhaps my favorite painting technique to create a watercolor effect is to make wide sweeping brush-strokes with many different colors to create a large, abstract—and this is the technical term—paint blob.

TIP I use my left hand to secure the fabric while I paint, but you can use painter's tape if you prefer.

1. Pick your color palette. I chose teal, blue, yellow, magenta, and ocher.

2. Choose your first color, and then starting at the top left of your canvas, begin painting in a large downward-sweeping motion. Continue with the same motion to paint the left side of your canvas. Dip your brush in paint as needed as you color the fabric. **(A)**

3. At the bottom, change to a different color. Use either the same brush or a different brush of the same size. If you want colors to mix, use the same

A

brush. Paint back up the canvas in a column next to the first color, making large upward-sweeping brushstrokes. **(B)**

4. Continue in this up and down fashion, changing colors at the end of a column, until you've covered the desired surface of your canvas. I like to cover the center area of my fabric, leaving about a 2-in. border without paint. **(C)** Before starting with a new color, feel free to add a few drops of water to dilute it.

5. While the paint is wet, go back and add details—more brushstrokes in different colors on top of already painted sections or drops of paint (shown). The larger the drop of paint, the larger the detail will be. **(D)**

6. Follow the package directions to let the paint dry (typically overnight). To speed-dry, use a hair dryer, or even take the fabric to an ironing board and, with a hot iron and ironing cloth on top, iron the fabric dry (see Tip on p. 74).

Thin brush: Fine details

Fine details will add depth and texture to your watercolor painting.

1. Using a fine brush, add fine details of your choice. **(E)** In my watercolor painting, I added several small circles and triangles (see p. 83). Any paint already on the fabric must be completely dry because any dampness will cause the paint to run.

2. Follow the package directions to let your watercolor dry (typically overnight).

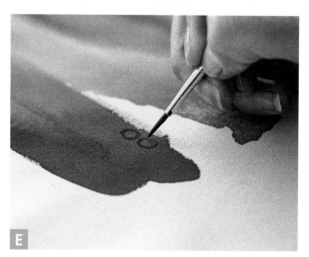

TIP To ensure that paint is dry, set it with a hot iron. Place a pressing cloth on top of the painted area and, with the iron set on high, press for 2 to 3 minutes. Move the iron consistently over the painted area to avoid iron prints. The pressing cloth will soak up any excess paint.

Mixing paints on fabric

1. One of my favorite effects with watercolor is adding a different color paint to an already painted portion of my work. As long as the original paint is still wet or damp, the two paints will mix together and not run outside the original paint line! (This applies to Kona Natural fabric.) The first outer edge you paint should maintain its edge. The bigger the brush you use, the larger the mixed-color area will be.

2. Make sure you let your paint dry and that you heat-set it with an iron before moving on to quilting.

Stitch it

1. Baste your quilt sandwich according to the instructions on p. 20.

2. Set up your machine. Choose matching thread in the top and bobbin. I use Aurifil 50wt black in the top and bobbin. Use a darning foot, drop your feed dogs, and use finger grips (see p. 19). **(A)**

3. Begin stitching by following any of your painted lines. This is really "free" because there are no rules as to design or direction. Do whatever inspires you! **(B)**

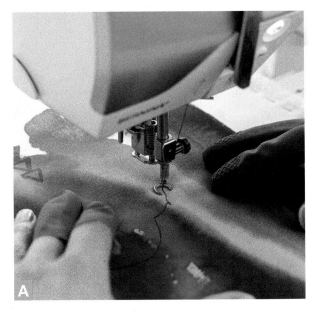

A

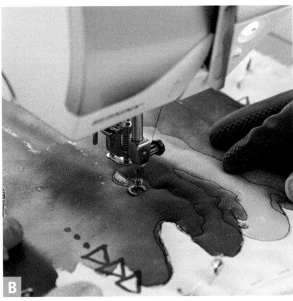

B

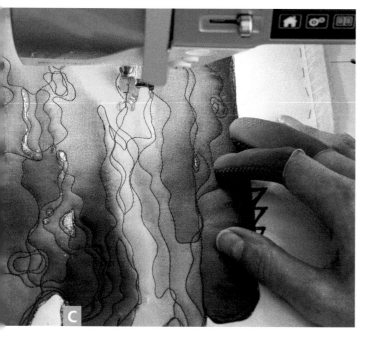

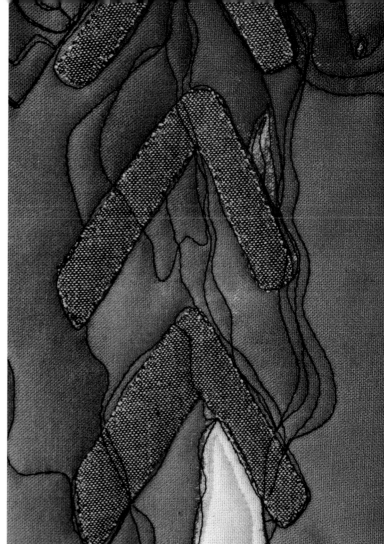

4. Quilt your painted surface, adding enough stitching to ensure that there is an evenness to the density of quilting. **(C)**

5. Add any background fillers to the unpainted portion of your quilt, which will give your project a finished look. See Lessons 3 and 4 for simple patterns. I like to use muslin or invisible thread so that the pattern I choose provides subtle background texture. On my example, I quilted around the painted design, about ¼ in. from the design's edge. If you like, you could also quilt a subtle pattern, such as pebbles, all the way to the edge of the quilt sandwich.

6. Finish your quilt following Lesson 7 (see p. 94).

Design Advice

After you have finished with the black thread, try using a different colored thread to quilt the painted area to add more depth or texture.

Add block lettering (see p. 80) to your design. Be sure to leave open space when you paint if you plan to do this.

RAW-EDGE APPLIQUÉ ON THE FLY

Appliqué is the technique of sewing layers of fabric to your quilt top, adding details and dimensionality to your work. Appliqué also allows you to add small, detailed pieces of fabric that might be too challenging to add through piecing techniques. Although appliqué has been around for centuries, it can be used to create a modern aesthetic.

Just as there are many options for appliqué shapes, from block letters to flowers to a shape replicating a fabric motif, there are also a few different appliqué techniques, but my favorite is raw-edge appliqué. This method is a quick-and-easy way to appliqué that doesn't require any edge-turning, hand-gluing, or hand-quilting.

It's important to keep in mind that all appliquéd pieces are fused to the quilt top *before* the quilting process, so *before* you baste together the three layers of the quilt sandwich.

- Spray starch
- Paper-backed fusible web (I like Soft Fuse brand)
- Iron
- Sewing machine with a blanket stitch or a zigzag stitch option
- Thread
- Background fabric
- Appliqué fabric
- Open appliqué foot (Bernina 20) (optional)

Tracing paper first

You might find a design you like that you want to trace with tracing paper first and then transfer to fusible web. Remember to reverse the tracing for asymmetrical designs.

Preparing to Appliqué

1. Spray-starch your background fabric to the stiffness of lightweight paper and let dry according to the manufacturer's directions.

2. Using a light box or window, trace individual appliqué shapes onto the paper side of the fusible web. Reverse the pattern for asymmetrical designs.

3. From the fusible web, cut out individual appliqué pieces ¼ in. outside of the pattern line. Depending on your design, you might need to cut the shapes as one piece, as I did; I'll cut these into individual chevrons once they are fused. If there is an interior shape in the pattern (for example, the inside of a letter R or the inner oval of a large oval ring), cut a scant ¼ in. on the inside of the pattern line to create edging. **(A)**

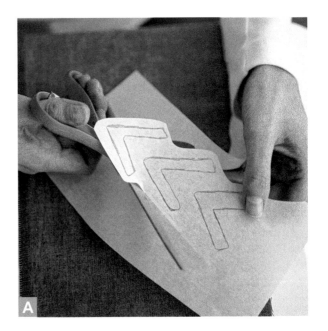

4. Fuse each appliqué piece to the back of the appliqué fabric, following the manufacturer's directions. **(B)**

5. Cut out the appliqué shape through the web and fabric layers on the pattern line. Also cut along any interior shapes in the pattern. **(C)**

6. Remove the paper from the back of the appliqué piece and place on the background fabric. Repeat until all appliqué pieces are cut out and positioned on the background fabric.

7. Fuse in place on the quilt top using a hot iron, following the manufacturer's directions. **(D)** Move the iron as you fuse the appliqué, which takes approximately 20 seconds.

Stitching Appliqué to the Quilt Top

1. Choose your thread. Use average-weight cotton thread in a color to match the appliqué or choose contrasting thread to highlight the appliqué. I like to use invisible thread. (In the photos shown below, I used yellow thread on top and gray thread in the bobbin to better demonstrate these steps.)

TIP Use the same color thread in the top and bobbin. If you choose invisible thread on top, use a neutral cotton in the bobbin.

2. Set up your machine with an open-toe appliqué foot. Use a single blanket stitch for raw-edge pieces. A general setting is a 2.0 stitch width and 2.0 stitch length. I use a smaller stitch width and length of around 1.5 because my chevron shapes are fairly small and I prefer that the stitches not take up too much space.

3. Start along a straight edge of your appliqué piece, if possible, with your needle off the appliqué piece. Follow the edge of the appliqué and let the "teeth" of the stitch come in on top of the appliqué piece. **(A)** If you need to stop stitching, make sure the needle is in the down position.

4. To pivot around a curved edge, stop with your needle down on the outside portion of the stitch teeth, then lift your presser foot and pivot the piece slightly. **(B)** Lower the presser foot and continue stitching.

TIP If you do not have a blanket stitch, you can use a zigzag stitch to create a similar effect.

5. On the corner, position the needle down, raise the presser foot, pivot your piece to 45 degrees, and make one complete stitch. Then pivot another 45 degrees and continue stitching. **(C)**

6. When you've reached your starting point, stop. Bring both front threads through to the back. There will be four threads. Neatly tie off. **(D)**

7. Follow these steps to sew down all of the appliquéd pieces. Once done, your quilt is ready for basting and quilting.

Basting and Quilting

1. Baste your quilt sandwich according to the instructions on p. 20.

2. Set up your machine. Choose matching thread in the top and bobbin. I use Aurifil 50wt black thread. Use a darning foot, drop your feed dogs, and put on finger grips (see p. 19).

3. Begin stitching by following the lines of the watercolor paint. It is up to you whether you stitch into the appliqué design or not.

C

TIP For secure stitches, you want your needle to be in the down position exactly at the corner. If it isn't, adjust your stitch length so that it is.

D

Transfer the Design

1. Write the word LOVE in block letters on a piece of paper, then trace it onto tracing paper. Make it the size you'll want to quilt it.

2. Turn the tracing paper over and outline the word several times with a lead pencil. Don't apply too much pressure or the paper might tear.

3. Turn the paper over so the front is facing up. Applying pressure, trace the word LOVE onto your quilt top. This will transfer some of the lead onto the fabric. If you have a light-color quilt top, you will not need to press very hard to transfer the lead. **(A)**

Stitch it

1. Begin free-motion quilting with the letter L. Start at the bottom left corner and stitch around the letter as shown. Don't forget your security stitches! **(B)**

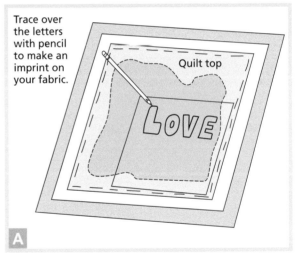

Trace over the letters with pencil to make an imprint on your fabric.

Quilt top

A

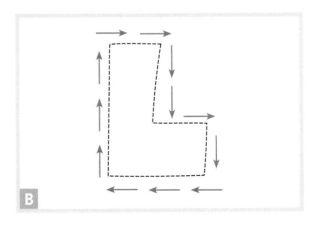

B

FREE-MOTION BLOCK LETTERING

I'm a font nerd. I have always been interested in typography. As early as I can remember, I enjoyed making block letters. You needed a sign? I was going to make it using giant, boxy block letters! You wanted them to be three-dimensional? Even better. It was only a matter of time before I figured out how to translate this *type* of writing (pun intended!) into a quilting technique.

Since free-motion quilting is similar to writing without picking up your pencil, quilting cursive words is straightforward, since letters flow from one to the next without stopping, cutting threads, and starting again. Thankfully with block letters, we can easily flow from one to the next by creating a subtle traveling line at the bottom of the text. Consider this line similar to the line you'd follow on a piece of lined paper. Let's practice!

TRACE AND PRACTICE

Practice first by tracing these block letters without picking up your pencil. You'll notice that any letter with a closed counter—the technical term for the closed central negative space area in letters such as A and R—needs to have one small travel line.

ABCDEFGHIJKLMN

OPQRSTUVWXYZ

2. After the L is completely stitched, travel to the O by stitching back over the bottom of the L and then stitching a straight line to the bottom of the O. **(C)**

3. Stitch the outside of the O as shown. When you reach the starting line of stitching, stitch a straight line to the closed counter (the inside of the O) and form that shape as shown. **(D)** I like to

stitch in a clockwise direction, but you can stitch counterclockwise if that is more comfortable for you.

4. Stitch back over the O as needed to get to the bottom of the letter and then stitch a straight line over to start the V. **(E)**

5. Follow the diagram to stitch the V and then the E. Don't forget to end with security stitches. **(F)**

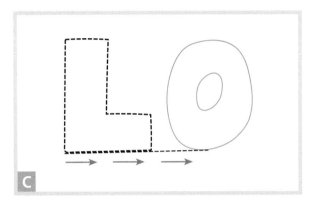

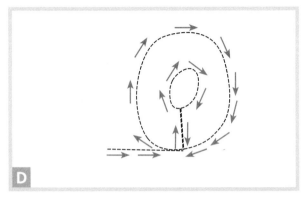

Design Advice

Once you're comfortable traveling between letters, vary the size and shape based on where you're stitching on your quilt top.

Wall Hanging

This project incorporates all three techniques used in this lesson: fabric painting, appliqué, and block letters. You may choose to do all three or omit one or two. My project is 14 in. square, but the size is flexible, so make it larger or smaller to fit your design.

It is a good idea to plan the composition of your piece in advance, or at least have an idea of how you'd like to appliqué it. I am a big fan of adding appliqué shapes that are informed by the painted areas. Therefore, I wait to plan my appliqué until I have painted my design. The same goes for my block lettering. I may have an idea for a word or phrase to include, but the final layout will not be decided until I see where the appliqué is located and the overall composition of the painted portion. In other words, the composition of this wall hanging emerges as you create!

- One 14-in. square of Robert Kaufman Kona Natural fabric
- One 15-in. square of batting
- One 16-in. square of backing fabric
- Dye-Na-Flow paint in colors of your choice
- Paintbrushes—at least a 1-in. brush and a fine brush
- Fabric for appliqué (small scraps, depending on your design)
- Ice cube tray or other palette for mixing paint
- 2 jars of water
- Paper towels and drop cloth
- Tracing paper and pencil
- Spray starch
- Fusible web (enough to make all appliqué shapes)
- Black thread
- Sewing machine attachments: darning foot for free-motion quilting and regular foot for appliqué

Paint the Design

1. Paint your square of Kona Natural with Dye-Na-Flow, following the instructions on pp. 72–75. For this piece, I created a large abstract blob pattern in the background and used a 1-in. brush.

2. Let dry, and then heat-set using a hot iron.

3. Add a second layer of paint. For this layer, I painted connected triangles using a fine brush. **(A)**

4. Let dry, and then heat-set using a hot iron.

Appliqué

5. Take a look at your painted piece to determine your appliqué shapes. For this design, I created appliqué pieces to cover several portions of the large sweeping columns.

6. Follow the instructions for Preparing to Appliqué on pp. 76–77 to make your appliqué shapes.

7. Stitch the appliqué shapes to the quilt top, following the instructions on pp. 78–79.

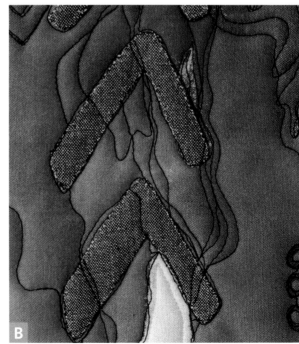

Quilt the Painted and Appliquéd Piece

8. Prepare your quilt for quilting: Make the quilt sandwich (see p. 20) and baste (see p. 79).

9. Using black thread, quilt your painted areas according to the instructions on pp. 74–75. When you approach an appliquéd piece, you may either quilt over it or around it. **(B)** Be sure to leave an open space within your quilted design to allow for any block letters you might want to add. **(C)**

Add Block Letters

10. Following the instructions on pp. 80–82, plan and transfer your block letters to your quilt. **(D), (E)**

11. Quilt the letters using black thread. **(F)**

Finish Your Piece

12. Refer to Lesson 7 on p. 94 for instructions on how to block and bind your quilt. For this quilt, you'll need 66 in. of binding tape.

13. If you'd like, add a label and/or hanging sleeve to the back of your quilt. See p. 102 for instructions.

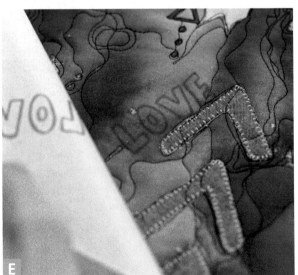

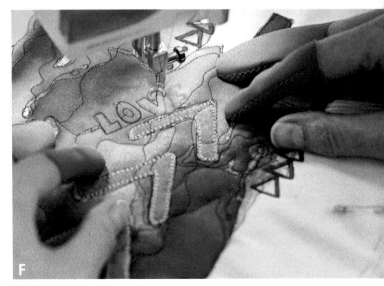

Lesson 6

SUNSET PICNIC BLANKET

It is time to put all of your quilting practice to good use with this full-size quilting project. There is relatively little piecing for this quilt top, which will allow you to focus on the machine quilting you have been practicing. This is a versatile quilt that can be used as a picnic blanket, throw, or even a twin bed quilt. The finished size is approximately 59 in. by 70 in.

If this is your first time making a large quilt, be patient and allow yourself time and space to construct and baste the quilt sandwich. Then focus on each segment as you go—first piecing and then quilting. Just as with any big goal, breaking it down into smaller, more manageable chunks is the way to avoid feeling overwhelmed.

MATERIALS AND SUPPLIES

For this quilt top, I used five different solid colors. Here is the yardage that you will need for each of the different sections, according to the diagram location:

- ¾ yd. each Fabrics 1, 2, and 4
- ½ yd. Fabric 3
- 1¾ yd. Fabric 5
- 4 yd. backing fabric
- 63-in. by 73-in. piece of batting (I use an 80/20 blend but use what you like)
- ½ yd. binding fabric
- Thread: 50/3ply for piecing; your choice for quilting (for ideas about color choice, see the tip on p. 89)
- Sewing machine attachments: walking foot for straight-line quilting and darning foot for free-motion quilting

Note: The yardage requires piecing together two pieces for each strip to maximize fabric usage. If you would rather avoid the seam, you'll need to buy 1¾ yd. of Fabrics 1–5; although 1¾ yd. means you'll have leftovers, I like to err on the side of having a little extra to allow for any fabric store cutting errors.

Cut and Piece the Quilt Top

1. Using a rotary cutter and mat, cut the strips for your quilt top as follows:

From Fabrics 1, 2, and 4:

- Cut two long rectangles that are the width of the fabric off the bolt (usually 42 in. after cutting off the selvage) by 12½ in.
- Cut one of the rectangles to 18½ in. by 12½ in.
- Sew the two pieces together, right sides facing, using a ¼-in. seam. Press the seam open. You'll have a strip that is 60 in. by 12½ in.

From Fabric 3:

- Cut two long rectangles that are the length of the fabric off the bolt (usually 42 in. after cutting of the selvage) by 8½ in.
- Cut one of the rectangles to 18½ in. by 8½ in.
- Sew the two pieces together, right sides facing, using a ¼-in. seam. Press the seam open. You'll have a strip that is 60 in. by 8½ in.

From Fabric 5:

- Cut one large rectangle that is 60 in. by 26½ in.

2. Piece all the strips together according to the layout in the illustration on p. 88 using ¼-in. seams. Press all seams open. The quilt top will now measure 70½ in. by 60 in.

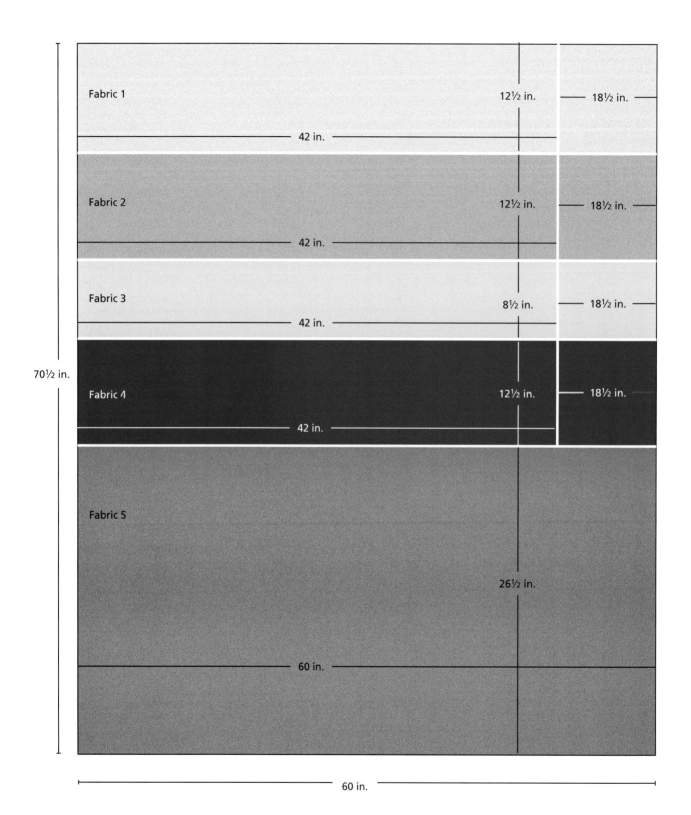

Fabric 1   12½ in.   18½ in.

42 in.

Fabric 2   12½ in.   18½ in.

42 in.

Fabric 3   8½ in.   18½ in.

42 in.

Fabric 4   12½ in.   18½ in.

42 in.

Fabric 5

26½ in.

60 in.

70½ in.

60 in.

Cut and Piece the Backing

3. Cut your backing fabric into two 2-yd. pieces, then cut off the selvage edge on both. Your pieces will be approximately 42 in. by 74 in.

4. With right sides facing, sew two of the long edges together, using a ¼-in. seam. Press the seam open.

5. Your backing will be approximately 83½ in. by 72 in. Cut it down so that it's about 75 in. by 65 in. **(A)**

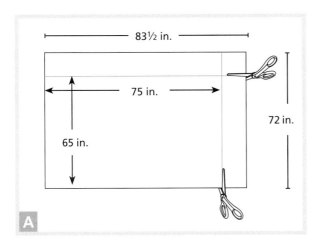

Plan and Mark Your Quilting

6. Before you baste your quilt sandwich, you should mark your quilt top, if desired. Once you have three layers and pins in the quilt top, it will be more difficult to draw on with a marking pencil.

7. For this quilt, I used five different designs from this book, one in each strip. In Fabric 1 (Pink Flesh), I quilted the Traveling Spirals motif; in Fabric 2 (Curry), I quilted the Pebbles motif; in Fabric 3 (Aqua), I quilted four rows of Whale Tails; in Fabric 4 (Ultramarine), I quilted Geometric Swirls; and in Fabric 5 (Tangerine), I quilted Daisies. **(B)**

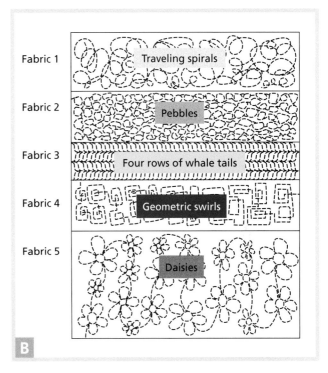

TIP Pick your favorite fabrics or color palette. My five-color palette reminds me of springtime magnolias and camellias in the park. I prefer solids for a more modern feel and also because they allow the various quilting patterns to take center stage. A low-volume print for the backing adds a bit of variety and provides a playful contrast with the quilt top. If you're looking for color ideas, play around with the color wheel or use a color-finding app like Adobe Color (color.adobe.com/create/color-wheel) or Design Seeds (design-seeds.com).

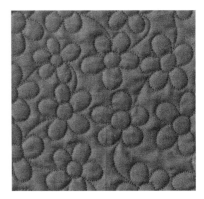

TIP If you'd rather not mix five different quilting patterns in this quilt, choose just one motif, such as Daisies. This is also a more simple approach, so if you're an absolute beginner, consider this option.

Baste Your Quilt Sandwich

8. Lay your backing fabric right side down on a large flat surface (I like to use the floor) and gently tape it down with a couple of pieces of blue painter's tape or masking tape. Make sure there are no wrinkles or loose threads stuck to the fabric.

9. Carefully place the batting down on top of the backing fabric, centering it and smoothing it gently with your hands. Check that there are no wrinkles or loose threads stuck to the batting.

10. Place your quilt top right side up on top of the batting. Center the quilt top and smooth it gently with your hands as you go. This is your quilt sandwich. **(C)**

11. Pin-baste the entire quilt sandwich, placing pins approximately every 3 in. to 4 in. Follow the instructions on p. 20 for details on pin-basting.

12. Using a sewing needle and thread, hand-baste around the perimeter of the quilt. (For more on hand-basting, see p. 20.)

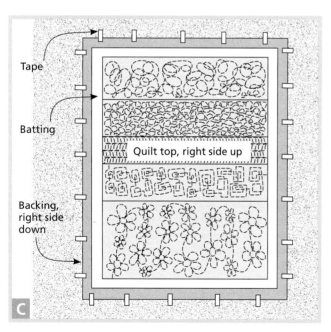

Tape

Batting

Quilt top, right side up

Backing, right side down

C

Choosing thread for quilting

If you would like your quilting designs to blend in and create a more subtle effect, use thread that matches the quilt top fabrics. If you chose one or more patterned fabrics, match the thread color to the dominant color in the pattern.

With fabric in hand, match threads at your local quilt shop or by using a thread color card. I use Aurifil thread and match the color to my fabrics with the color chart found at aurifil.com; it has 270 colors to choose from!

I chose to use the same thread throughout this entire quilt—a soft neutral tone that will not stand out too much (Aurifil 2605). For beginners, this is easier than changing thread colors multiple times during the course of quilting. If you'd like to do the same, keep in mind that your thread will not match every fabric. The back of the quilt will have a more textured effect than colorful effect as well.

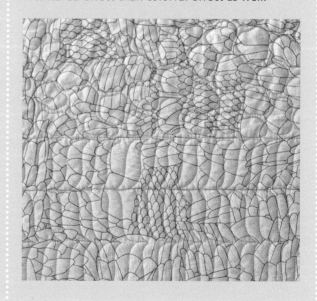

Quilting

If you have basted your quilt well, you should be able to begin quilting anywhere. However, when I am quilting a larger quilt, like this one, I like to start my quilting in the middle so that I have a manageable amount of rolled-up quilt. (Rolling up the quilt, called packaging the quilt, is discussed on p. 27.) If you are working band by band (meaning you have chosen 5 different quilting motifs like I have), I recommend turn the quilt 45 degrees so that your quilting will begin from top to bottom of the strip. This means that your new "top" is actually one of the east or west edges if your quilt had a directional axis. **(D)** Each time you finish a section, take your quilt out and repackage it to prepare for the next section.

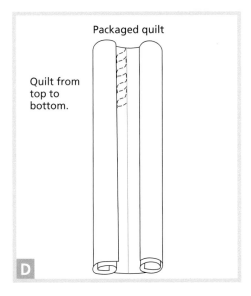

Packaged quilt

Quilt from top to bottom.

D

13. Find your starting spot and begin quilting either section by section or until your quilt top is evenly quilted with one motif. Be careful that you remove safety pins as you go so you do not quilt over them.

Finish Your Quilt

14. Block your quilt following the instructions on p. 95. After blocking, your quilt should be approximately 70 in. by 59 in.

15. Make binding strips from the ½ yd. of fabric by following the instructions on p. 96. You should have a strip that is approximately 270 in. long.

What can go wrong when quilting

- Threads break or you run out of thread mid-quilting. Don't worry! Simply remove a few stitches until you have a tail long enough to tie off on the back of the quilt. Then, begin quilting again at the point where your design has stopped.

- Bunching or folding of the fabric. If the bunching or fold is small, it won't show up very much, so don't worry about it. If you'd rather, you can remove some stitches to fix it and then restart. Or you could quilt over it, which would disguise it. Major bunching or a large fold that will be noticeable should be fixed. One way of determining this is to slide your fingers over the top of the quilt. If the area feels like a significant bump, I recommend removing a portion of the stitches with a seam ripper and starting again. Once you start quilting again, try to distribute the quilt top material evenly to diminish the bunching.

16. Attach the binding to your quilt following the instructions on p. 97.

17. Add a label to commemorate this quilt (see p. 102).

PART THREE

Finishing Your Quilt

LESSON 7: Blocking, Binding, and Finishing

Lesson 7

BLOCKING, BINDING, AND FINISHING

Finishing your quilt properly is equally as important as making your quilt properly. Blocking your quilt and adding a binding are the finishing touches to ensure that your quilt will lie flat, whether it's hanging on a wall or spread across a bed.

There is a lot of information available about how to block and bind your quilt, but I encourage you to use this section as a reference for finishing any of the projects in this book, as well as any other quilt you make.

Blocking Your Quilt

With all the packaging of your quilt during the quilting process, it's common for the quilt to be slightly distorted and wavy. Blocking your quilt can easily fix these issues.

1. Lay your quilt right side up on the carpeted floor and smooth out. Using T-pins, fasten your quilt to the carpet, placing the pins in the space between your quilting design and the raw edge of the quilt top. **(A)**

2. As you continue pinning around the quilt top, pull your quilt taut but not so hard that you create holes in it where the pins are placed.

3. Lay the pressing cloth over the area of the quilt you will press first, then spritz the area with a light mist of water from a spray bottle. If your quilt is small, your pressing cloth may cover the whole quilt. If the quilt is larger than your pressing cloth, start in one corner of your quilt and work around the surface. **(B)**

4. Press with a hot iron. Pressing involves placing your iron down firmly and then lifting it up again to move it from one area to the next. Do not push and drag the iron over the surface, as this may create distortion.

5. If needed, move the pressing cloth to another area of the quilt and repeat this process until you've pressed the whole quilt.

6. Your quilt will be slightly damp after pressing. Allow it to dry fully by leaving it flat for 4 to 6 hours or even overnight.

7. Once your quilt is dry and flat, remove the pins.

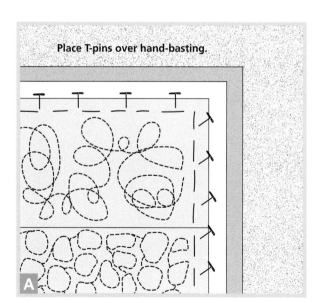

Place T-pins over hand-basting.

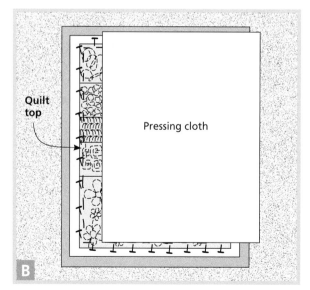

Quilt top

Pressing cloth

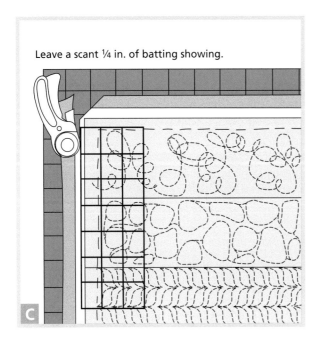

Leave a scant ¼ in. of batting showing.

C

8. Place your quilt on a cutting mat. Beginning at one corner, cut a 45-degree angle and then cut down the side, leaving a scant ¼ in. of batting and backing showing on the edge. Use a ruler to help guide your rotary cutter. **(C)**

9. Cut the next three corners and sides in the same way, moving the cutting mat under the quilt as you go. Be sure that each corner is a 45-degree angle and each side is evenly cut. Your quilt is now ready to bind.

TIP There is no need to remove the hand-basting before blocking the quilt; however, it is easier to remove this stitching before you attach the binding. If your quilt top is not heavily quilted toward the edge of the quilt, I recommend leaving the hand-basting and attaching the binding on top of it. You may even cover it completely with your binding.

Binding Your Quilt

There are several ways to bind your quilt. I am going to share three different ways—single binding, double binding, and a quick machine-stitch binding. Single and double binding are traditional quilting techniques; machine-stitch binding is my favorite trick for wall hangings or art quilts.

Making single binding

A single binding is made up of one layer of fabric. You will typically use single binding if you want a finer, more subtle binding or for quilts that will not get a lot of use such as wall hangings or quilts that are for display.

1. To make single binding, you will need a strip of fabric that is 1¼ in. wide. To determine the length of this strip, measure the perimeter of your quilt and then add 10 in. For example, a quilt that is 14 in. square has a perimeter of 56 in., so the strip needs to be 66 in. long (56 in. + 10 in. = 66 in).

2. To make binding that is longer than 42 in., which is the width of quilting cotton, you'll need to piece strips together. Cut the ends of two (or more) fabric strips on a 45-degree angle, pin, and then sew them right sides together with a ¼-in. seam. **(D)** Press the seam open and trim the fabric tabs. **(E)**

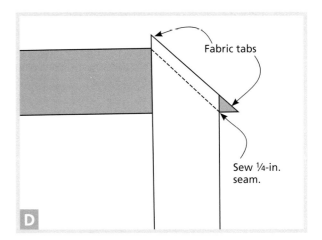

Fabric tabs

Sew ¼-in. seam.

D

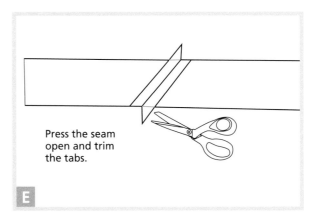

Press the seam open and trim the tabs.

E

Making double binding

Double binding is made up of a double layer of fabric. It creates a heavier, more durable binding and is normally used on bed quilts, throws, baby blankets, or any quilt that will be used heavily and washed often.

1. To make double binding, you will need a strip of fabric that is 2½ in. wide. To determine the length of this band, measure the perimeter of your quilt, and then add 10 inches. For example, a quilt that is a 14 in. square has a perimeter of 56 in., so the band needs to be 66 in. long (56 in. + 10 in. = 66 in).

2. To make binding that is longer than 42 in., which is the width of quilting cotton, you'll need to piece strips together. Cut the ends of two (or more) fabric strips on a 45-degree angle, pin, and then sew them right sides together with a ¼-in. seam.

3. Using a hot iron, press the strip in half lengthwise with wrong sides facing in. **(F)** If you haven't already, press the seam open and trim the fabric tabs (see illustration E on the facing page).

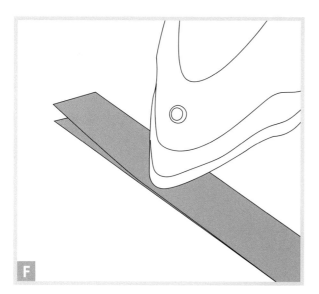

Attaching single or double binding to your quilt

1. Leaving about a 4-in. tail, align the edge of the binding with one edge of the quilt top, with right sides facing. Starting about 4 in. from one corner, pin your binding and quilt top together until you reach another corner. **(G)**

2. Using your walking foot, machine-sew the binding with a ¼-in. seam until you're about 3 in. from the corner. Stop stitching with the needle in the down position. **(H)**

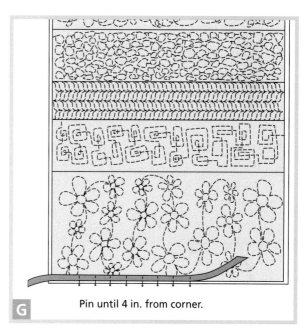

Pin until 4 in. from corner.

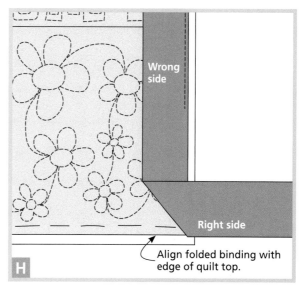

Wrong side

Right side

Align folded binding with edge of quilt top.

Fold over to create tab.

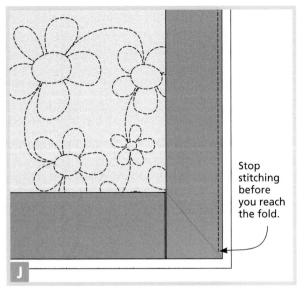

Stop stitching before you reach the fold.

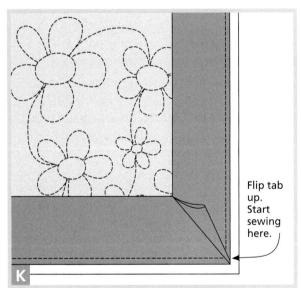

Flip tab up. Start sewing here.

3. To prepare the corner, fold the binding over to the right at the same line as your quilt top (as shown in illustration H on p. 97), then fold it back toward the quilt. Fold the triangle-shaped tab down. **(I)**

4. Continue sewing until you reach the point where the folded area begins. Stop stitching before you reach the diagonal fold. **(J)**

5. Take your quilt out of the machine (don't cut the threads) and turn it 45 degrees. Fold the triangle-shaped tab up. Begin sewing at the point where the tab folds up. **(K)**

6. Continue attaching the binding along the next side. Stop when you are 3 in. from the corner and prepare the next corner (see steps 3-5).

7. Continue in the same manner until you have turned your fourth and final corner. Stop 6 in. to 8 in. from where you began stitching. Trim the tails so they are no longer than 8 in.

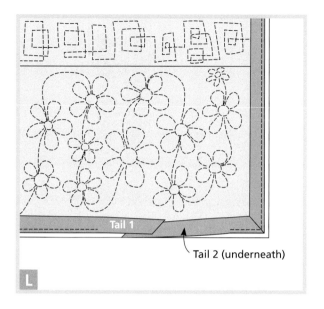

Tail 1

Tail 2 (underneath)

L

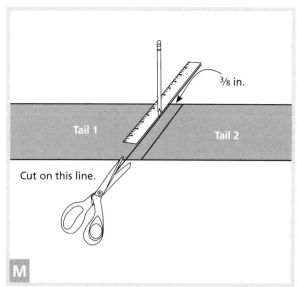

³⁄₈ in.

Tail 1

Tail 2

Cut on this line.

M

8. Cut the first tail—Tail 1—to a 45-degree angle. Position the second tail—Tail 2—along the edge of the quilt and then position Tail 1 on top of it. **(L)**

9. Using a pencil, mark the top and bottom of the binding strip where Tail 1 meets Tail 2. Then fold Tail 1 out of the way and use a ruler to draw a straight line connecting the two points on Tail 2.

10. Now draw another line ³⁄₈ in. to the left of the first line. Cut on this line to remove the tail. **(M)**

11. Fold the two tails together, right sides facing, forming a tab similar to those you made when joining the binding strips (see p. 96). Pin, then sew the tails together, using a ¹⁄₄-in. seam. **(N)**

12. Press the seam flat using a hot iron and trim the tabs.

13. Using your walking foot, finish attaching the binding tape along the perimeter of your quilt.

14. Now attach the binding to the back of your quilt with a blind stitch.

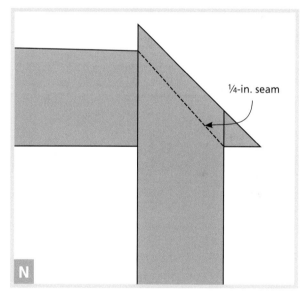

¹⁄₄-in. seam

N

....

TIP No matter whether you're using a single or double binding, work with only about an arm's length of thread when hand-finishing binding. Use thread that matches the binding to help hide the stitches.

....

SINGLE BINDING

15. If you've used a single binding, fold over about ¼ in. and pin to the back of the quilt. Work with only about 4 in. of binding at a time. **(O)**

16. Hold your quilt so that the bulk is falling away from you, with the quilt top facing down in your lap. Choose a starting place (not a corner) and secure your thread with a knot in an area where the binding will cover it.

17. Start making blind stitches, working from right to left. Be careful not to stitch through to the front of your quilt! Rethread your needle when you run out of thread and make another knot in an inconspicuous place. **(P)**

18. As you approach a corner, you'll need to form a miter. Use your needle or a pin to smooth the corner, so that the fold is at a flat 45-degree angle. Use blind stitches to secure this small seam. **(Q)**

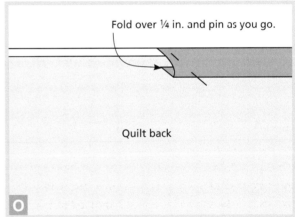

Fold over ¼ in. and pin as you go.

Quilt back

O

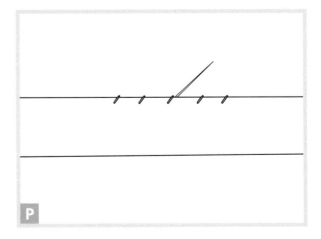

P

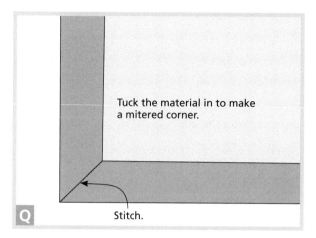

Tuck the material in to make a mitered corner.

Stitch.

Q

DOUBLE BINDING

19. If you've used double binding, simply fold the binding to the back of the quilt, pin, and hand-stitch a blind stitch to finish, following the instructions above.

TIP If your quilt will get heavy use, consider securing the binding corners through to the front of the quilt. Bring your needle through to the front then back through to the back with a couple of stitches, and then continue securing the binding along the next side.

Quick machine binding for wall-hanging quilts

Who doesn't love a shortcut? When I am making a series of small quilts that will hang on the wall, I do not need to be as precise about hiding all of the raw edges. This is why I will often use my "quick machine binding" trick to save time.

1. Cut, measure, and attach single binding following the instructions on pp. 96–100. Instead of folding over the binding ¼ in. and finishing with a blind stitch on the back of the quilt, fold the binding over to the back and leave the raw edge flat.

2. Pin around the perimeter of the quilt, tucking in the corners as you go (see step 18 on the facing page). **(R)**

3. Using your walking foot, sew a seam on the front of the quilt that is directly next to the binding—essentially stitch in the ditch but a thicker ditch since you're sewing two layers of binding versus a pieced seam. This will take some finesse and attention, but if you go slowly and use a matching thread, you will barely even notice this seam. **(S)**

4. When you've sewn along the perimeter, stop. Cut the threads, leaving a 2-in. to 3-in. tail. Pull the top threads through to the back and tie off.

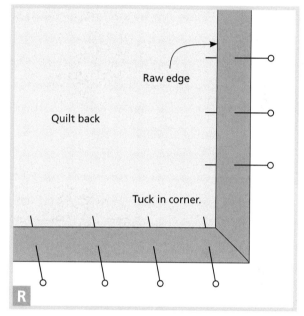

Raw edge

Quilt back

Tuck in corner.

R

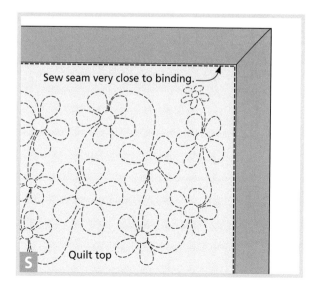

Sew seam very close to binding.

Quilt top

S

1. I like to practice my layout and composition of the details on paper first, then use a thin Sharpie or other permanent pen to write this information onto the fabric square, leaving about a ½-in. border. **(T)**

2. I fold over the ½-in. border and press with a hot iron, then pin the label to the bottom right corner of my quilt. A blind stitch around all four sides of the label secures it. **(U)**

T

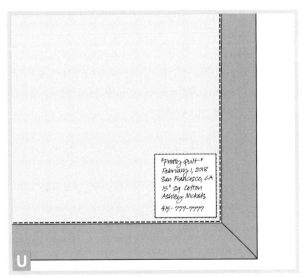

U

Adding a Label

It is always a good idea to add a label to your quilt. A label allows you to add your name to the quilt and include any identifying information about it, should it ever get lost. Even if your quilt is used for everyday purposes and will remain in your possession, labels are a good way to record when and where you made the quilt. If you're anything like me, you can never quite remember when you made a quilt! Writing this information on a fabric square is an ideal way to time-stamp your work.

The size of your fabric square will depend on how much information you want to include. I typically cut a square of fabric that is around 5 in. and include the following:

• Name of quilt
• Date it was made
• Where it was made
• Dimensions, materials, and any other information specific to the quilt
• My name
• My phone number (or email)

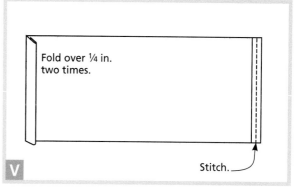

Fold over ¼ in.
two times.

Stitch.

V

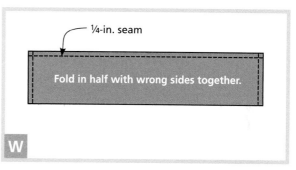

¼-in. seam

Fold in half with wrong sides together.

W

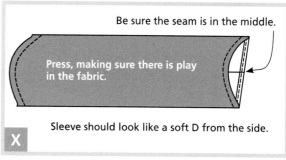

Be sure the seam is in the middle.

Press, making sure there is play in the fabric.

Sleeve should look like a soft D from the side.

X

Adding a Sleeve

Most quilts hung for display, either in your home or in an exhibit or show, use a wooden pole or rod. In order to hang your quilt with a pole or rod, you'll need to attach a sleeve. If you enter your quilt in any kind of exhibition or show, attaching a sleeve is a requirement.

The sleeve can be in the same material as the back or a different fabric. Since the sleeve doesn't show, you could even consider looking in your scrap bin for something the right size.

1. Cut a strip of fabric 8½ in. wide and the exact width of your quilt.

2. Working on one side at a time, fold the sleeve ends in twice ¼ in., so ¼ in. and then another ¼ in., and then stitch using a ¼-in. seam allowance. **(V)**

3. Fold the long side of the sleeve in half, wrong sides together, and sew a ¼-in. seam. **(W)** Press the seam open and position the sleeve so that the joining seam is in the center of one side; press. The seam side will face the quilt back.

4. Position the sleeve seam side down. Press the top long edge, then press the bottom long edge, leaving a bit of play in the fabric before pressing the bottom edge. The rod will push the sleeve inward, which is why you need to leave some play in the fabric. **(X)**

5. Pin your sleeve along the back of your quilt, positioning it about ½ in. to ¾ in. from the top edge of the quilt (including the binding) to ensure that the sleeve will not show from the front once it is hung. Using a blind stitch, attach your sleeve to the quilt back along both edges.

TIP Be mindful that you don't catch the front of the quilt as you're stitching the sleeve to the back.

GLOSSARY

Appliqué: A fabric cutout that is layered onto another piece of fabric, usually with some type of fusible web.

Backing fabric: Fabric used for the back side of the quilt. Usually consists of large yardage pieced together, though can also be more intricately pieced.

Basting: Process of temporarily securing the three layers of the quilt top (called the quilt sandwich) for the quilting process. Basting can be done by hand by making large stitches, by using pins, or by spray basting.

Batting: Fluffy material used in the middle of the quilt sandwich. Batting can be cotton, polyester, wool, bamboo, or blends.

Binding: The finished edge of your quilt, usually made with handmade or store-bought binding tape.

Blind stitch: A hand stitch used to secure the binding to the back of the quilt. Also used to attach a hanging sleeve or label.

Blocking: Process of squaring and flattening the quilt after the quilting process in preparation for attaching the binding.

Bobbin: The circular spool of thread found in the bottom of the sewing machine. Bobbin thread is fed through the throat plate and is grabbed by the needle, which is threaded with the top thread, to create quilting.

Feed dogs: Metal "claws" that emerge from the sewing machine throat plate that help pull the layers of fabric through the sewing machine as you sew.

Free-motion quilting: Stitching a quilt sandwich on a sewing machine without feed dogs.

Hand-basting stitch: A hand-stitched seam around the perimeter of the quilt sandwich in preparation for quilting. This stitching secures the edge of the quilt top so it will not move during quilting.

Hanging sleeve: A fabric sleeve stitched to the back of a quilt that holds a wooden or metal rod so the quilt can be hung for display.

Ironing: Running your iron across the surface of the fabric to remove wrinkles. *See also* Pressing.

Marking: Using a pencil or washable pen to draw lines or patterns on the quilt top as guides for the quilting process.

Packaging the quilt: Rolling or folding the bulk of your quilt during the quilting process so it fits into the sewing machine area.

Presser foot: An attachment on the sewing machine that holds fabric as it is fed through the machine and stitched. The most common presser feet for free-motion quilting are the free-motion quilting foot, walking foot, and open- and closed-toe darning foot.

Pressing: Patting your iron in an up-and-down motion on top of a seam, appliquéd piece, or other section of patchwork to set the fabric. *See also* Ironing.

Quilt: a bed covering or wall hanging consisting of three layers (two outer layers of fabric plus an inner filling, usually of batting) that has stitched designs to fasten the three layers. Also, to stitch designs through layers of material.

Quilt sandwich: Refers to the three layers of the quilt: two layers of fabric (the bread) and batting on the inside (the meat).

Quilt top: The fabric or pieced fabric used for the top of the quilt sandwich. Very often it is pieced, though it can be "whole cloth," meaning the same fabric is used throughout.

Quilting cotton: Fabric made specifically for quilting. Quilting cotton tends to be stiffer than apparel sewing cotton.

Rotary cutter: a.k.a. the "pizza cutter." A very sharp rolling cutting device used to cut precise pieces for quilting.

Seam allowance: How much space you leave between your stitched seam and the edge of your fabric. Common seam allowances are ¼ in. (for piecing in quilting) and ⅜ in. (for garment sewing).

Seam ripper: A sharp metal device used to cut through a sewn seam to expedite the process of taking out a length of stitching.

Security stitches: Stitches very close together to secure the beginning and ending of stitching.

Selvage: The tightly woven edge of the fabric, usually containing product and color information. On a solid, the selvage may blend in and can be identified due to its uneven or frayed edge. If in doubt, try to unravel the threads of the fabric; if you can't, then you've identified the selvage.

Start anywhere motif: A quilting pattern that doesn't require you to start stitching at a particular point.

Stitch length: How far apart your stitches will be when you sew on your machine. Usually set at 2.5 millimeters automatically, stitch length can be adjusted. When you drop the feed dogs (as you do for free-motion quilting), stitch length is created manually.

Tension: Refers to the evenness of stitching. Correct tension on your sewing machine means that stitching looks the same on both the top and back of your quilt.

Throat plate: The part of the sewing machine directly below the presser foot, where the feed dogs are found.

Yardage: The amount of fabric you'll need for a project.

INDEX